MW01063422

THE MAGIC TOUCH

How to Make $100,000 per Year
as a Massage Therapist

MEAGAN HOLUB L.M.T.

Olive Vine Press
Seattle, Washington

Published by Olive Vine Press
117 E. Louisa St. #449, Seattle WA 98102

Cover and book design by Studio 5 Design, Seattle, Washington

ISBN: 978-0-9823655-0-2

What good is money without sharing it?

A percentage of proceeds from the Magic Touch
will be donated to the following non-profit organizations:

www.kidsdonations.org
www.childhaven.org
www.freeartsnyc.org

For Teri Adolfo, MTCM, L.Ac
Whose intuition and the gift of a book, lead me to my destiny.

For my friends who went above and beyond.
You know who you are.
This book is as much yours as it is mine.

For the clients who shared advice, stories and admissions.
My success would not be possible without your generosity.

I am truly blessed to have every one of you in my life.

CONTENTS

FOREWORD
(or why I wrote this book)

In the fourteen years that I have been a Massage Therapist, I have never had a mentor who was in the same profession as myself. I suffered and was very poor for many of those years, and felt helpless and confused about where to turn for advice or guidance. At times I felt like there must be secrets to earning a living, however small, that other Massage Therapists must know but would not share with me.

Like many of you, I looked for guidance in the books that were available. The pioneering books in our profession were thorough, but often contained too much information for me to get through without feeling overwhelmed. They were great reference manuals, but they generally were not personal enough to inspire me. I felt little connection between what I was reading and my own circumstances. I scoured the bookshelves looking for the book that would explain in detail how to be a successful and prosperous

Massage Therapist. By the time I finished reading yet another book I just felt discouraged all over again. I repeatedly found myself thinking, "I don't have the money to start up my own business," or, "I haven't been practicing long enough to be successful." These negative thoughts went through my mind more than I care to admit.

On top of this lack of basic business know-how, I struggled with low self-esteem from a few less-than-desirable experiences at massage school and in the workplace. I was confused about whether or not I was "worthy" of being a healer, and even more so about whether or not it was okay to accept money for my gift. I even believed for some time that to succeed I would have to tone down my outspoken personality, hide any hint of my physical attractiveness, and drastically alter my personal style. Basically, I thought I would have to diminish myself in order to fit in and be a "good" Massage Therapist. It is a miracle that I somehow kept a stubborn enough resolve to begin to earn a bare basic income and lifestyle while staying true to my sense of who I am. I believe this is partly due to the fact that there is so little inspirational information in print, or otherwise, that describes in honest and straightforward terms how to make a great living at this profession.

Spas, chiropractors, and cookie-cutter massage companies often pay therapists 10% of what they charge the client. New therapists accept these rates feeling that $10, $20, or $30 an hour is an acceptable rate, or simply feel they can't complain. It is understood that there is always an eager new face to fill a void.

The reality is that therapists working in these situations rarely work more than a few years before burning out. No one can sustain a pace of seven massages a day forever. Either they find themselves with repetitive stress injuries or simply can't continue giving away their energy day in and day out. The flip side of this is that the client doesn't get 100% any longer. And they feel it. They often go looking elsewhere for a new therapist before the original therapist inevitably leaves. What a terrible, vicious cycle for both the therapist and the client. This is not the scenario I want for you. I want you to be adequately compensated for the gift you give the world.

Massage therapy is a noble career choice. Out of all the careers in the world, we have committed to something that is deeply healing, and often profoundly transformative. Unfortunately, there is no way of documenting or proving the incredibly positive changes I have seen regular massage bring to my clients' lives. But they are real. More than once I have seen people change careers, begin a new exercise program, exit an unhealthy relationship, and go back to college to finish that long-forgotten degree (all at the same time!). I have witnessed billionaires come up with the next multi million-dollar idea. In fact, I have one client who aims to get a massage every day and attributes many of his light bulb moments to just that. I have witnessed emotional outpours that finally allowed a stubborn three-year backache to let go. I have witnessed a twenty four year old find relief from chemotherapy treatments. I have seen over-exposed and, as a result, neurotic, celebrities trust a stranger with deep, dark secrets. I have seen auto accident victims recover from pain they believed was going to debilitate them for life. You need to know and understand the power that lives within your nurturing touch. You need to be adequately compensated for that power. *The Magic Touch* will give you the knowledge you need to do both.

In writing this book, I am not going to cover any of the

basic massage school curriculums. If you have not yet graduated from a reputable massage school and been adequately certified and licensed at a state and national level, I will trust that you are on your way to doing so. Or perhaps you are currently a Massage Therapist working for someone else and frustrated with being paid little to nothing. Or maybe you are one of the brave MTs who have ventured out on your own without achieving the satisfaction you had hoped for. All of those are excellent starting points for the guidance in this book, guidance based on my own success in the massage industry.

In a city rumored to be the most competitive for Massage Therapists in the world, with an impressive 2,500 massage students graduating, I have done something I previously did not know could be accomplished. I have learned the secrets to earning $100,000 or more a year working less than twenty hours a week. I have developed a reputation as Seattle's celebrity Massage Therapist. I have built a massage company that, in just six months and on a $600 advertising budget, was asked to provide exclusive service for four major hotels. I have lived out of the country for six months on income earned through this same company. And now I have written this book. Not a bad résumé. Would you believe, from start to finish, the bulk of what I built took just three years? Furthermore, would you believe that I did it mostly by looking at what was currently not being done well within the industry? I'll bet you haven't heard that before. I'll bet you haven't heard a few of the things I'm about to tell you.

In the upcoming chapters I'm going to give you the secrets of my own success as a Licensed Massage Therapist. But I ask you to do something for me in exchange: suspend your judgment. Trust that I am here to help you by providing you with honest stories and observations about how I have gone from broke and unhappy to successful and living the life I love. To get here I had to ask a lot of questions, step out of my comfort zone in trying new ideas and, most importantly, I had to take action. To succeed, it was necessary for me to take action against all odds and all my deepest fears.

It won't take you three years to become as successful as you aim to be. You will have this book to steer you clear of all the mistakes that I, and others before you, have made. As I said before: suspend judgment. You may not like my honesty, my stories, my choices, but they are what moved me from a life of poverty and misery to one of happiness and prosperity. I urge you to ask yourself: "What have I got to gain?" Read until the end. It's not terribly long. I can't wait for you to tell me wild tales of your successes.

"You must be the change you wish

to see in the world."

\- Mahatma Gandhi

1

RUBS TO RICHES

Have you dreamt of working half the hours of the average North American, while earning twice the average income? Or have you imagined being named one of the "best Massage Therapists in the world" by celebrities, power players, and professional athletes? Ever dared to dream of the advantages of living the celebrity lifestyle while you travel with your favorite VIP? Have you ever wondered about developing a thriving medical massage practice, one that sustains you through a tough economy? Or maybe you've daydreamed of living in another country while contracted Massage Therapists earn income for you? These are examples of the career I have been fortunate enough to build, and the life I have been grateful to live. Now I feel it is time to give back to the profession that which I have been given. My goal is to arm you with knowledge; to teach you every thing I have learned in over fourteen years in this industry. My sincere desire is that this knowledge will guide you towards the success of YOUR dreams.

Although the last half of my career as a Massage Therapist was as good as it gets, I was not so fortunate for the first half. Those years were ones of hardship, financial struggle and physical exhaustion. I often felt that I was much like a hamster on a wheel. I was tired of making the same mistakes and getting no further, but hadn't the knowledge I needed to change my unfortunate circumstances. Round and round I ran, until one day I couldn't run any further. I was simply too exhausted. I had become bedridden with fevers. My life had become nothing more than massaging from morning until night and sleeping away the rest of my free time. Whether I had risen to top position at a world-famous spa, prestigious country club or small chiropractor's office, it brought the same result: exhaustion, fevers and never enough money to pay rent on my tiny studio apartment.

The truth of why I was debilitated by pain and fatigue after each workday was a secret that I kept for many years, for fear that others would not believe me. The truth was that I could not only feel my clients' pain, but I would take it from them and carry it in my own body. Understandably, I was afraid of people's reactions. I wasn't strong enough for the criticism and disbelief I feared I would receive. So silently, carrying other's burdens, I would return home each day with the headache from my first client, pain under my scapula from my last client, and all the pain from every client in between. My clients would marvel at how I "knew". They'd walk into the treatment room and I'd say, "You have a headache behind your right eye today." And they would reply, "Yes! Is it that obvious?" (As if I could SEE a headache.) In fact, I was feeling the pain behind my own eye. On top of all this, I was scared that the very thing that was making me sick, my empathy, was the only reason I was a gifted Massage Therapist. On some level I believed that if I found a way to protect myself from others' pain, that it would result in a loss of my intuition; the same intuition that guided my touch. I convinced myself that to be a healer in this world you must suffer.

Looking back, I see how I was an enabler from a very young age. Massage was a way for me to get praise and connection from people that I wasn't getting from my family. By the time I was in my mid twenties I didn't know any other way to be. I gave, gave, gave and surrounded myself with people who took as much as they could get from me, tired and sick as I was. Deciding to become a Massage Therapist was just par for the course. I was giving more than I had to feel loved and appreciated in every other aspect of my life, as well.

I first discovered massage at the young age of fifteen. I was riding home from school on the bus, when my best friend asked me "Have you ever had anyone do pressure points on you?" I hadn't a clue what pressure points were. But I compliantly passed over my right hand. What happened next changed my life: I felt my entire body almost melt. I felt instantaneous bliss from head to toe. My posture relaxed, my eyelids drooped. I no longer felt the familiar tug of self-consciousness through my teenage body. I almost felt as if I was floating; like I had slipped out the window of that clunky old school bus and drifted into the clouds. I was hooked.

I begged her to massage the other hand. Then I insisted she massage both my hands repeatedly and I returned the favor. I excitedly asked her "What exactly are pressure points? How does it work? How does rubbing only your hand relax the whole body?" She couldn't answer any of my questions, but I was determined to find the answer to every last one.

With my newly found passion, throughout high school I was the girl who massaged everyone I could get my hands on. I would sit on the couch, they would sit on the floor in front of me, and I would work my magic on their backs, necks, and scalps. I became quite popular at parties. My classmates would line up around the room and down the hallway to wait their turns. I remember one kid saying to me "You are so great at this, Meagan. I bet one day you'll massage movie stars!" I remember replying something sarcastic like, "Yah, right. I'll never get out of this town. You think I'll make it to Beverly Hills?" But in the back of my mind I thought, "Me. Massaging movie stars. It could happen."

I quickly learned that massaging and caring for others would get me praise that I desperately needed. So I began to build a life around just that. I volunteered at Camp Easter Seal during summer breaks, became the youngest Physical Therapist Assistant in Washington State, and moved in with a paraplegic at just seventeen, as a live-in aide, while simultaneously escaping a less-than-desirable home life.

And so my habit of enabling snowballed until my mid twenties; at which time I literally couldn't get out of bed because I was so sick. I wasn't just physically ill, I was sick of life. I was sick and tired of being hit on by men who flaunted crass and lewd behavior. I was tired of being mistreated by friends and loved ones who tried to make me feel I never gave enough. I was tired of strangers stopping me on the street to complain of their current life-crisis. I was especially tired of giving my gift of touch and intuition to greedy corporate entities that didn't care whether I lived or died, much less whether I was happy and healthy or fainting from exhaustion.

One day something clicked inside me. I suddenly understood that it didn't matter how many times I tried to protect myself from others' pain in the massage room, if I was collecting it from every damaged soul I came across in my daily life. I realized in this same moment that my poverty, my fatigue, lewd treatment from others, disrespect from friends, all of it stemmed from a lack of personal boundaries. This lack of personal boundaries stemmed a root problem: low self-esteem.

From that day forward I began to develop my personal boundaries. I asked toxic people to exit my life. I imagined a bubble around me as I walked down the street. As a result, I no longer had strangers downloading their pain on to me. I no longer experienced lewd or violating treatment from men in or out of the massage treatment room. Nor did I have clients' aches and pains clinging to me after each session. And most importantly, I began a quick ascent of building my own business and charging top dollar for what I give to the world.

I thought I was alone all those years, but I see so many of you are in similar situations in that many of you feel fatigued, under-appreciated, under-paid, and at a loss for where to turn. Many of you give, give, give, only to have nothing left for you. This is not the life that you want. I know how you can get the life you do want, and the life you deserve. It starts with you creating boundaries for yourself, both personally and professionally. The reality is that I didn't have to live through such difficult and exhausting situations to earn a decent income. And neither do you.

Establish boundaries in your life. Learn how to say "no". This may be a difficult habit to break, but after seeing the immense benefits that your new way of being brings to your life and business, it is so worth it. The truth is you cannot be any real benefit to your clients, family, or friends if you are an enabler.

To prepare you for any unexpected or uncomfortable situations that may arise in this profession, I have provided a list of challenging situations from my own career as an LMT, following this chapter. I suggest you spend a fair amount of time studying each example. Visualize each situation occurring during one of your massage sessions. Note your immediate reaction. Is your instinct a fight or flight response? Is your reaction to shut down and avoid the situation altogether? Or even to pretend it's not happening?

Now with an awareness of your initial reaction, search for the more mature, professional response if there is one. Seek a solution that protects your boundaries while reflecting your personal integrity and enhancing your self-esteem. If any of these scenarios I have provided for you bring about feelings of discomfort that feel unmanageable, enlist advice or guidance from a trusted resource. Massage school instructors, successful long term Licensed Massage Therapists, and counselors will typically have the tools to talk you through the fear and help you find an empowering solution. The point of this exercise is to find your place of empowerment and assure your preparedness when walking into a massage treatment room, whatever may await you. The irony is when you are prepared, and you enter the treatment room with well-defined boundaries and confidence, these types of situations will rarely, if ever, happen. Defining your boundaries creates less need for you to have them in the first place. Just as I, for the last half of my career, have felt rejuvenated after each and every massage and no longer carry the pain of others within me, so shall you feel the velocity of ascent to the career of your dreams increase with each well-defined boundary you implement for yourself and your business.

Choosing to be self-respecting and someone who remains true to your ethics in this profession will not only further your ascent to success much faster, it will also guarantee the advancement of the average person's respect for our chosen profession. This, in turn, will increase the world's massage awareness. I can think of few careers that are more important to people's well being than massage therapy. You and your fellow Massage Therapists deserve to be recognized and compensated for the gift you give the world. And the world deserves to receive the gift of healing touch from you.

Visualization Exercise

What would your professional response be to the following:

A client has a panic attack during a session.

You discover a malignant case of melanoma on a client.

You and a client have an unspoken crush on one another.

An LMT slanders your reputation to other professionals in your city.

An obese client asks you to explain why he is in so much pain.

A competing company copies 75% of your ad content and design.

A client purposefully pushes his draping aside and exposes himself.

A famous religious leader asks you to accept his religion.

Your complaint of sexual harassment leads to 50% fewer referrals.

A pro athlete invites you to an all expense paid vacation.

You suspect that a client has been misdiagnosed.

A client insists that you reveal whom you voted for President.

You discover a large parasite under the skin of a client.

A celebrity offers "any amount of money" for a full release massage.

A client trips while getting off the table and lands with his head in the wall.

"He who has health has hope; and he who has hope has everything."

- Arabic Proverb

2

WEALTH WITHOUT HEALTH
IS WASTED

One of the biggest epiphanies I had during my fourteen years as a Massage Therapist is that the more I take care of myself, the more I can take care of others. We've been told this so many times it's become a cliché. "You can't take care of others without taking care of yourself." Even so, my experience has been that the true healers attracted to this profession have the hardest time learning this lesson. Many get burned out before they are able to start experiencing the joys and freedom this profession can bring. It saddens me that those of you who have the strongest desire to help, and are sensitive and intuitive enough to do just that, often struggle with caring for yourselves. You give everything away only to have nothing left, and sadly nothing to show for your contribution. I am on a mission to see more natural-born healers find success as Massage Therapists; to become not only prosperous, but also respected, with full well-balanced lives. This chapter is intended to help guide you towards greater health, both physically and emotionally. Always remember that this is a journey that we do not walk alone. Every one of us is in the process of healing or maintaining health in body and mind.

I first discovered how crucial being in touch with my body and maintaining my physical wellbeing was by nearly flunking out of massage school. My wake up call should have been sparked by the countless times that I'd tried to retain information taught in class, only to have it leak out of my memory like water down the drain. Whereas previously I got top grades without ever cracking open a book. Or it should have tipped me off that something was terribly wrong when I would awake in the morning debilitated by pain from my neck to my hips, and that pain stayed with me until I went to bed at night, when I would toss and turn, but rarely sleep. You'd think one of these events would have alerted me that something was not quite right with my body. But sadly, it wasn't until a specialist in chronic pain came to massage class to lecture on the symptoms of living with chronic pain until I began to catalog my own symptoms one by one. It was like someone had flipped a switch inside me. I began to cry in the middle of the lecture. I had blocked myself from my own pain for an entire year. In that year I had been suffering acute pain and brain trauma following a major car accident. While it would take me years and a few seizures to uncover the brain trauma, the bodily pain was alerting me in every way that it possibly could to get help. I had instead pushed the pain as far away from my awareness as possible. I was working full time, going to school full time, and needed to heal myself full time. The reality was that I was barely holding my job together, was about to flunk out of massage school, and was in indescribable pain.

It took me years of pushing my body past its new limits to finally come to a place of balance. For many years I would skyrocket to the top position of whatever spa or country club I was working for, only to give more than I have and end up having to quit because of terrible fevers and body aches. My body's hypersensitivity to an overzealous workload necessitated by a less than adequate financial compensation added with an inability to disassociate myself from my clients' pain was debilitating, and I would not wish it upon my worst enemy. However, it is ultimately what made me begin to recognize how fragile the human mind-body is. It was this realization that began my search for the ways to work fewer hours and make more money in this profession. The secrets that I will be revealing to you were discovered through the necessity of my own survival.

I have revealed these very personal truths for you to understand that for me, living a balanced life and practicing rituals of self-care is not just an ideal. Without it, I would not be able to succeed. It was a long journey from the fateful day of my auto accident to find a balance of health for my own body. It required patience and dedication. Likewise, if you would like to be successful at this profession for many years, finding your balance and maintaining a healthy lifestyle is a necessity. None of us is immune to ill health. Whether it is caused by illness, accidents, or reversing the effects of time as we age, we all have put forth effort to maintain a pain-free body.

There are a few rituals that I would like you to consider practicing for health and longevity as a masseuse every day. I feel these methods kept me providing deep tissue massage for fourteen years without injury. First, before you begin your day, stretch for ten minutes. This way no matter what comes up in your day—stress, too much work, five loads of laundry, little time for a workout—you have had ten minutes of YOU time. This is also a perfect time to visualize goals and intended accomplishments. Stretching sets a positive tone to the upcoming day, gets musculature, joints, and nervous system moving with ease, and calms and centers the mind. I've found it helps my attitude remain upbeat if I have practiced self-care that morning.

Every evening, before bed, practice anti-inflammatory rituals. Ice your wrists (or hands, elbows, or thumb—whatever you use most in your treatment of clients). I find this helps immensely with reducing risk of repetitive stress injuries that could pose a major threat to MTs' ability to work. In this profession it is all too common for us to lose our ability to provide for ourselves because of carpal tunnel, tennis elbow, and arthritic fingers.

Keep your energy level at top performance. Figure out what foods keep your blood sugar up, and carry them with you.

Drink enough water during the day that you don't feel like a horse in the desert after each massage (but not so much that you can't focus on the client because your bladder is demanding all your attention). Take Epsom salt baths regularly. The magnesium sulfates will absorb into your skin and reduce inflammation. Effective homeopathic prevention methods include taking Bromelain, a pineapple extract that is a powerful anti-inflammatory, and adding a B-complex vitamin to your daily diet. Be sure to consult your health care provider for suitable doses for your body and lifestyle.

Besides stretching and using proper body mechanics during massage treatment sessions, find activities that keep your joints mobile and muscle tissue healthy and strong. I recommend yoga, swimming, dance, Pilates, Tai Chi and/or cycling. If you have any chronic injuries, I suggest you hire or trade with an injury specialist personal trainer. They will guide you toward safe and effective techniques for your particular set of needs.

And finally, take advantage of the myriad of other body workers and Eastern medicine treatments available to you. One of the best things about being a healer is that many other healers will be eager to trade sessions with you. This means, hypothetically, you can trade your massage dollar for dollar or hour for hour to receive acupuncture, chiropractic, iridology, reflexology, hypnotherapy, yoga, dance instruction or guided meditation, as examples. You may also have the opportunity to trade with MTs who offer different types of massage therapy or energy work. So, while you are building a community and establishing trust with referrals, you are also keeping your mind-body finely tuned and without disease. Moreover, the better you get to know these other modalities and philosophies, the better you will be at referring your clients to healers whose techniques will combine effectively with your massage.

Not only did I uncover my physical needs during that fateful lecture, but it also became clear that I had emotional pain buried within that needed to be addressed. The two are never separate entities. What the body feels so does the mind. Many mentors in this business stress the importance of Massage Therapists taking care of themselves, physically, to prevent burnout. I was personally never told that many people attracted to the healing arts are in need of a good dose of emotional healing as well. It is the nature of healing. Those who need it are attracted to it. Hence, more than a few damaged souls end up in massage school.

Many of you have been physically hurt or injured. Many of you have had to be the caretakers in your family for a variety of reasons. Many of you have been abused physically, emotionally, psychologically, or sexually. All this is going to come up for you as you are in the process of healing others. You have to be ready to deal with your baggage, because in this industry there is nowhere to hide. You are going to be exposed to people's darkest and deepest fears. It is shocking and hurtful, for example, the first few times other Massage Therapists are threatened by your abilities. You must learn to quickly move past it. You cannot let others get in the way of your own journey.

Similarly, clients will sometimes present challenges. You must realize it's not personal. Physical injuries, especially traumatic ones, can bring out all sorts of fears and reactions in people. Be prepared. It's true that Massage Therapy is a healing art, but it is still a business. Have a plan of action that is mature and professional.

Clients will even try to cross professional lines in ways that feel deeply personal. At some point, a client will make a pass at you, ask you on a date, or do something that feels violating. Let that client go if you need to. You have to be healthy enough to walk away guilt, blame, and anger free. Be honest with yourself about your needs and frailties as they arise. Trying to pretend there isn't a problem could potentially attract these same scenarios to you over and over again, until either you feel you are going mad or you finally deal with the underlying issue.

Bottom line: heal yourself. Utilize counseling services if you need them. Learn to create all types of unbendable boundaries. Anyone who asks you to bend them more than once is not someone you need in your life. I don't want you to think you can't trust people because generally you can. What I am trying to relay is that your unresolved issues can and will come up in this profession. Life has a funny way of hitting you over the head with painful stuff until you make it less painful for yourself. If you want to be successful at helping people, you have to first help yourself.

And please don't mistake what I am saying here. You do not need to be 100% baggage-free before you become a Licensed Massage Therapist. I don't know anyone that doesn't have something within themselves that could use a little healing. Arguably this is the journey of life. Each day provides you with bountiful opportunities to heal, grow, and become more of your most creative, contributive force in this world. With each painful experience, or unexpected detour, that arises you are being offered a fast track to personal evolution. So, take a deep breath when these things arise and walk into them head high and eyes open. It will get a bit easier each time.

I once had an enlightening conversation on this subject with a much-respected journalist a mere few hours before she interviewed the Dalai Lama. What she said to me I wish someone had told me fourteen years ago: "What most people don't understand is that to be a healer in this world, amidst so much pain and suffering, you must find the balance between keeping an open heart—being profoundly empathetic—and being a warrior. No one ever tells you that to do good and bring peace and progress into this world you must fight. But fight you must. You must be strong, or you will not make it." She knew, as I know, as you must also know, that a life of healing will take everything from you if you let it. And then the world would have one less light to guide the way. You taking care of you is the only way you will be able to reap the astounding benefits of being a positive force in this world.

"The intuitive mind is a sacred gift and the rational mind is a faithful servant. We have created a society that honors the servant and has forgotten the gift."

- Albert Einstein

3

FIND YOUR MAGIC TOUCH

Throughout the years of my career I have heard "that was the best massage I have ever had," from my clients, more times than I can remember. Typically this comment is followed by the client explaining what makes he/ she an "expert" in massage. They've said, "I have had massages around the world in all the best resorts and spas", and, "I have been getting massage regularly for thirty years from only the best therapists", and even, "I've seen Oprah's masseuse on occasion, and you are better than him". (Wow. What a compliment! Oprah hires only the best, I could only DREAM to aspire to such heights!) These comments have been a regular occurrence for me from some of the world's biggest celebrities, politicians, and athletes.

While these types of comments have, of course, been thrilling, from time to time I have felt humbled and confused by them. I find myself pondering the same question over and over.

"What makes one massage better than another?" This is a question that plagued me throughout my entire career. Quite honestly, I am surrounded by Licensed Massage Therapists with more knowledge of anatomy than me. I have worked with LMTs who are geniuses in getting their clients aches and pains to release. I have witnessed LMTs' clients nearly walk into walls after their massage, because they were so relaxed. So what was it in my hand, my touch, my table-side manner that made me rise to the top of the client's phone book, every time? I have had clients ask, "What is it about your touch that feels so different from every other Massage Therapist?" They have asked how I know exactly where they hurt, how to touch them, and when to ease up. My reply is always the same: "It's my intuition."

According to the Myers Briggs personality test, the most respected test of its kind since the 1940s, only 25% of the population is intuitive in nature. The other 75% are sensory in nature. These sensory people like to trust what they see right in front of them, and like to believe what past experiences have proven to be true. Whereas the intuitive bunch, well... they trust something else entirely. For some of these people it's a hunch, a vision, a gut feeling. Some have physical reactions; see colors, smell things or feel physically compelled towards or away from a situation. For many it's simply a knowing. Commonly, intuition is defined as a knowing that is derived from the subconscious. But that only seems to be true for some. I know of one popular reality television star who claims to speak to the "spirit guides" of her guest stars. She claims this is the way she solves the problems of these guests' family situations. How she discovers problems that have happened in the family that have long been forgotten, but are still creating tension and dis-ease. This is all very "behind the scenes", of course. The show represents her abilities as those of an ordinary woman with a gift for child rearing and family psychology. She is one of many successful people I have met who relied heavily on intuition to bring them to where they are today.

In truth, the more I admit to others that I am an intuitive individual the more I realize that many great people are and were. Einstein spoke of the power of intuition much more than most people realize. Many people assume because he was a great man of science, that he couldn't possibly have been an intuitive person. But despite a societal majority that may not understand this gift, people are sharing their unique ways of knowing with those who will listen, scientists included. In fact, without intuition many of our current technologies would not exist. The television was dreamt of by a fourteen-year-old named Philo Farnsworth, while he was tilling rows of potatoes. During that tilling he came up with the idea of shooting electrons past rows of images where it could be seen on a box: a television. How did an under-educated potato farmer's son come up with an idea like that? We'll never know how much of it was genius, and how much of it was intuition. But the story reads like a modern-day fairy tale. In truth, every day someone saves a life because they had a "vision" of disaster, every day a CEO of a major corporation makes a decision that gains millions for the company based on a hunch, and each and every day a healer knows exactly what to give to ease a person's suffering through the use of this gift.

A small portion of this 25% is destined to be a Massage Therapist. Some are destined to be composers, artists, authors, homeopaths, teachers or any number of other noble professions.

Each of us has a unique set of personality traits developed throughout our lifetime. Life's trials and tribulations provide you with daily reasons to become more of who you are. If you are intuitive, you know you are. It is something you do not have to wonder about. It has always been with you. It has made you an outcast at times. By now you have most likely realized that if you don't follow your intuition, no good comes of it. So there are times that you appear to act without reason. At the very least, you are considered a unique individual. Likewise, if you are one of the sensory-based individuals, by now you know it. You were born this way. It is who you are. No amount of pretending to be intuitive, or surrounding yourself with intuitive people, or reading books about intuition will make you someone else. In fact, you will be denying yourself of yourself. And really, there is so little time to waste being anyone else. We all need to be who we are in this world to effect the change that we are here to effect.

What does all this have to do with giving a great massage? You will give a great massage once you accept what your gift is. If your gift is intuitive in nature, develop it. Test your intuition on a daily basis, and note the results. Enlist people to help you develop this skill through tests of your design. Make sure these people are truly honest with you and themselves during these exercises. It doesn't do you any good if your friends agree with you to be "nice". You won't develop your skill that way. If you are a sensory person, examine what is it is that draws you towards this profession. What is the element that excites you about working with the human body? Is it the results you see after working with an injured patient? Is it that you feel deeply curious about human anatomy? Is it that you admire the human form of athletes in top condition? Tap into your true motives. Be steadfast in aligning yourself with the part of it that makes you most passionate. Market yourself with this goal in mind. Do not take a job at a spa when you are only interested in working with athletes, for example. Find your niche and go for it.

Though it's true that my intuition has helped get me where I am today, I am chagrined with the massage experts who advise sensory-based students to spend significant amounts of time developing their intuition. Certainly this is a great place to put your energy if you are already someone who perceives the world in an intuitive way. But in my humble opinion, people who do not perceive the world this way would do better to enhance the ways in which they do see the world. There is room for both personality types in this industry. The sensory-oriented individuals will often be the MTs who draw the majority of new clients into trying a massage with their more traditional ways of viewing the world. They will often be the ones who build respect for this profession with doctors and health insurance companies. They will typically be the ones who can explain with textbook efficiency why massage is a successful medium for reducing pain and healing musculature injuries. You sensory-oriented Massage Therapists are invaluable for the growth of this industry. The key is in knowing who you are, and accepting those strengths versus trying to develop those that are foreign to you. If you do this, your path to success will be an easy one. Not only in this profession but whatever you aim to achieve.

Likewise, if you are an intuitive person, do not be afraid of the way in which you "know". Each and every time I give a massage, my hands are drawn to places of injury like magnets. I can describe what the adhesion buried under a knot in a client's erectors feels like before I touch his or her body. I know exactly how to bend my elbow to a point, and slide it next to that person's spine (without touching it) with a gentle pressure to access and release that spot. I also know that the moment before it releases it sends a pain referral into the right side of their temporal region. I am aware of the moment when it is time for me to stop applying pressure to a low back that refuses to release, and instead place my hands on the body, quiet my mind, the client will burst out into tears... and the pain will disappear. I know many of these things, the feeling of the pain, the description of it, in part, because I have carried my own pain for the last fourteen years. But much more of this knowledge is gift whose origins remain unknown. I may never know where this knowledge comes from. For many years I have been humbled and awed by this mysterious quality that is surely in all of us, but is so tremendously powerful in few of us. If you are an intuitive person, listen to what guides you and never look back. At times you may be misunderstood. Less intuitive people may find you to be irresponsible, irrational, or even arrogant. But if your intentions are pure, you need not care. Do not take an entire lifetime to learn that it is not your business what other people think of you. Your business is the business of healing; and this starts with you. And the only way you can do that is to BE yourself.

Whichever modalities of massage you put your interest, develop skills outside of the basics your school provided you! If you are currently following a scripted massage treatment plan (start at the toes, five minutes each foot, this stroke, that stroke), break away from it immediately. Start by giving your client what they ask for. If they want you to focus the majority of time on their feet, their neck or their glutes... do it. If they ask you to work light, deep or anything in between... do it. Feel free to work on any connected muscles that you feel are also affected, and antagonist muscles, but let them know why. If you give them what they want the first time, you will later have a next time to explain to them that massaging the whole body is ideal. If you don't, you won't have a next time. They'll find someone who will acknowledge their needs. I know of a seven-year old girl who really drove this point home for me. She had been getting massage since she was a baby. After explaining to me that she no longer let Massage Therapists, other than me, give her massage because "they hurt her", she added "Those Massage Therapists need to learn how to not push into people's knots so hard, or they will never see that person again. They only have the first time to get it right." I marvel at how a seven year old could see this so clearly. She was not only appalled at these MTs' lack of attention toward her, but also understood and was able to see the long term effect of displeasing clients creating a loss of repeat clients. If she, a seven-year-old can see this so clearly, it makes me that much more perplexed why many Massage Therapists don't understand this simple truth.

Give the clients what they want. Give them what they need. Whether they tell you what that is, or you intuit what that is. Give it to them. It is really that simple. Open yourself up to touch in your own life, so that you may be that much more understanding of what the client is feeling. Watch the body's reactions. Often the body will tense up if something is wrong. Intertwine flowing, relaxing strokes with your treatment work. The mind and body seem to respond to treatment much faster when you coax it gently in between the Deep Tissue. This brings me to a misperception about Deep Tissue application that I feel I must address. It is the "harder is better" theory. Not only are there many Massage Therapists spreading this theory, but now there are just as many clients believing the "no pain, no gain" theory. I've had clients who brag about being bruised and tell me there is no way I can get as deep as they need me to. Whenever I hear this, I immediately know that the client has not yet had a massage with a highly intuitive LMT. If they had, they would know that it takes very little pressure to reach the pain threshold when the exact area of pain is addressed. What they have previously experienced is more likely a Massage Therapist burying their elbow into generalized areas of muscle tissue, creating a desire for more pressure because the areas of pain have not yet been released, thus creating a cycle of deeper massage in healthy muscle bellies, while injured muscle tissue remains mostly ignored.

With these clients, I never give the pressure that they are asking for immediately. I am already drawn to the exact sites of pain, so to bury the point of my elbow into it would send the client reeling off the table. Instead, I slowly sink into the area, checking in with the client along the way. They are typically shocked and impressed that I barely need to apply pressure (I use about 5% of my strength) to get them to where they are saying "enough!" I never take their "you can't possibly go deep enough for me" attitude as a challenge. If I did, I would hurt them, and that would be totally unacceptable. Instead, I take it as an opportunity to educate my client about effective Deep Tissue techniques. They are typically blown away. The results have already proven themselves, so they are open to listening and typically ask, "If so little pressure is needed to provide better relief, why have I been told all this time that more pressure is better?" My answer is always, "The Massage Therapists you have been working with are most likely lacking either intuition or proper training. They don't know where the damaged muscle tissue is located, so they cannot treat it with precision. They compensate by going deeper into the muscle bellies. But now you know the difference between an educated Deep Tissue Massage, and one that is not."

Another misperception about Deep Tissue Massage application is the idea that an adhesion, knot, or hyper tense muscle should be worked on ceaselessly until it releases. I can explain why this doesn't work. Both the body and mind need frequent breaks from pressure or friction being applied to an area that is injured. Without these breaks, the body, and especially the mind, is unable to remain relaxed on the intense level that is required for the site to release and melt away. If the treatment is painful up to the point where the pain threshold is met, and there hasn't been a "coaxing" of the tissue along the way to release, it typically won't.

Deep Tissue Massage is a bit like a man trying to get a shy woman to go on a date with him. He must stroke her mind with soft kind words, to get her guard down in between applying pressure for the result he wants to achieve: the date. This may take some time, and a few rounds of gentle coaxing. If he were to just pressure her, without the kindness, she would back away and put up a wall of resistance (and possibly get a restraining order on him). The body's responses are much the same. When the pressure applied to a sensitive area begins to surpass the line of "hurts so good" to just plain "hurts" I begin applying Swedish Massage strokes. Usually by the third pass over a site of pain with this method, the pain is relieved.

There are strokes that seem to "trick" the mind body into relaxing, as well. I see many Massage Therapists using only Direct Pressure to release areas of hypertension. While there is a time and place for all modalities, I have found that Cross Fiber Friction, even on large knots, can be very effective in pain relief. The back and forth stroke seems to create a quick reaction in the client's mind of "that kind of hurts, oh no it doesn't, yes it does, no it doesn't..." which allows the area to be treated much longer and with more efficiency than if the LMT were just pressing on the area. The brain registers direct, unceasing pressure as "This hurts. This hurts. This hurts..." This is the body's natural response when being hurt for any amount of time, same as the metaphorical girl who was being chased for a date, which is to back away and put up defenses. This is the exact opposite of what we want to have happen. We want to ease into the tissue with whatever tactic works for the particular body we are working with so that the body can release with ease and comfort.

A more common client complaint is a total lack of Deep Tissue application on the part of Massage Therapists that are marketing themselves as Deep Tissue Massage Therapists. The only thing worse than a massage that is too aggressive, because of a lack of intuiting where the sites of pain are located, or knowledge of how to treat them, is a massage that is too light for the same reason. If you are not able to easily intuit or palpate where people are sore to be able to give Deep Tissue massage that is effective, worry not. You have options. You can develop your abilities as a Swedish Massage Therapist, learn Lomi Lomi Massage, Thai Massage, Aromatherapy, Reflexology, or get very good at Myofascial Release Techniques, for example. There is a world of opportunities out there for you to build a niche market without misleading your clients about your abilities. I have repeatedly witnessed Massage Therapists reply "of course" when asked if they give Deep Tissue Massage and then refuse to go any deeper than Swedish Massage, despite their clients' pleas. This is utterly disgraceful behavior on our part. As professionals, we have an ethical duty to be forthright with our clients and to give them what we say we will. We have a duty to ourselves to remain in integrity, and keep our word at all times. It is not dishonorable to not give Deep Tissue Massage. Other modalities are equally as valuable, despite what some may say. What is dishonorable is saying you do something, accepting payment for that something and not doing it.

If you are not getting honest, positive feedback about your Deep Tissue Massage skills, and have no interest in further educating yourself in other types of massage... you are most likely in the wrong profession. I hate to be the one to break it to you. But believe me, you will never be successful at this if you are lacking intuition AND a passion for healing. My clients claim they can feel that these people are not healers, the minute they lay their hands on them. Many swear to me they can tell the minute they look the LMT in the eye. There is nothing worse than having to lie on a massage table while getting a terrible massage. Except, of course, being the one who is giving the massage, and hating every minute of it... that's pretty awful too. If this is you, save yourself the headache, hassle, time and money. Move on. Ask yourself what you REALLY want to do in this lifetime and do it. Consider yourself saved from losing more valuable time, money and resources on following the wrong path in life. You most likely know what you are truly passionate about. It is not this, and life is too short to be doing anything that you are not passionate about. You'll thank me for saying this when you are living a life you love.

For those of you who are passionate about developing your Deep Tissue skills, you have a large client base ready to take you into the fold. It has been the number one most requested modality everywhere I have worked, throughout all the years of my career. I feel a great explanation of how to access soft tissue through deep-tissue massage is presented in Deane Juhan's "Job's Body", in which the Gel-Sol Theory is explained. Not only do I feel every LMT should know of this theory, and understand how to apply it to their Deep Tissue Massage, so should each and every client ultimately know the generalities of this theory so that they may make an educated decision about whom they should be hiring to work with their bodies.

This theory states:

"There is no tissue in the body that is as ubiquitous as connective tissue, and as it migrates and develops in various locations, its 'connective' qualities cannot be overstated. It binds specific cells into tissues, tissues into organs, organs into systems, cements

muscles into bones, ties bones into joints wraps every nerve and every vessel, laces all internal structures firmly into place, and envelops the body as a whole. Taken as a whole, then, connective tissue in its various forms can be regarded as fluid crystal, a largely non-living material that can be adjusted over a wide range from sol to gel."

What this means in layman's terms, as far as Deep Tissue application is concerned, is that through manipulation such as massage, the body's tissues can turn from a solid state to one of more liquid or gel. This is especially observable with Deep Tissue Massage. Let's use Direct Pressure as an example. If you were to press your straightened fingers into a client's rhomboid without preparation, or warmth first delivered to the area, this theory impresses the idea that the tissue would respond by solidifying (gel). There would be resistance, and getting deeper into the tissue would require more pressure. Whereas if the rhomboid were accessed very slowly and incrementally as the tissue warmed up, the rhomboid would not only not resist, but would allow your fingers to "melt" into it as if it were now a liquid (sol) in place of a more solid muscle. While some people disagree with specifics of this theory, I feel that the basics of it are very sound and should be studied by each and every Massage Therapist. The tissue should indeed let you know when it is ready to accept you by turning an accessible consistency.

A fun and easy way for anyone to get an understanding of the tactile difference between sol and gel states is the "Non-Newtonian experiment". In this experiment you will be able to feel the difference, and witness the science behind liquids transforming from liquid to solid with nothing more than pressure applied. Quick sand is probably the most commonly known liquid of this type. And trying to walk through it is a great metaphor for working with the tissue. You push too hard, pull, fight your way out... you're stuck because the liquid turns solid. If you instead allow yourself to float to the top with little resistance, you will move through the quicksand with ease. Deep Tissue bodywork is much like this. Retain this knowledge as you train, and you will have the tools to become a great Massage Therapist, capable of delivering exceptional Deep Tissue Massage. To create this liquid called "ooblec" yourself, and play with different pressure speeds and amounts, is very simple. You need the following:

- Cornstarch (about 1/4 cup, or 60 cm3)
- Water (about 1/4 cup, or 60 cm3)
- A bowl for mixing

Mix the cornstarch and water into the bowl until the liquid has a firm texture to it when you manipulate it with your hand. You may need to add additional cornstarch to get it to its proper consistency, but you'll know when you find it. At that point you should be able to let the mixture pour through your fingers like liquid, but be able to roll the mixture into a solid ball. If you apply firm pressure to the top of the liquid it should feel solid. Play with different pressures. Notice how the liquid gives if you access it slowly, but if you press hard it solidifies. This is a great example of Deep Tissue Massage applied to the muscles. Try different strokes on the liquid, and notice the results.

There are quite a few Non-Newtonian experiments on youtube.com. One man showed how you can "walk on water" on the Ellen DeGeneres show with a small pool of this liquid. To find any one of these examples type "ooblec", "Non-Newtonian", "cornstarch and water magic", or "walk on water" into Google search. You'll be able to find people who have played with huge vats of ooblec, and it is truly amazing. Use every tool available to you, such as the aforementioned experiment, to provide a well-rounded development as an LMT.

Throughout your career as a Massage Therapist it is necessary to continue evolving and growing in abilities. For some, that means increasing the number of modalities they study. But to become master of any of them is a tremendous accomplishment. If you are particularly drawn to any specific modality of healing, I urge you to put the majority of your study into this one mode. Learn other things as well, and by all means, if other modalities intrigue you, add them to your repertoire, and divide your focus. But never confuse an excess of book-learned knowledge for being a great healer. Healing is partly instinctual, and the rest is learned through respect of the chosen medium. If you have memorized every word of every book ever written on massage, it does not make you a healer. If you have taken every massage class available to you, it does not necessarily mean that you are a healer either.

To be a healer you must have a deep and abiding respect for the human existence. You must have a deep curiosity for the healing abilities of the body and desire to participate in its wellness and recovery. The core of you, not only your surface self, must have an ability to be non-judgmental about the human body and mind in every one of its states of weaknesses and frailties. To be a healer, you must find any and all ways that the human body speaks to you and develop this gift. If you suspect that you have this gift... Know it. Embrace it. Nurture it. And evolve it. We need you in this world exactly where you are, doing exactly as you are doing. If you have fear, let it go. Transform it into motion. Take your fear and work with its momentum to learn every nuance of every stroke that makes you the best Massage Therapist that ever was. Harness that fear and market yourself with pride. If you are new at this, know that we all once were, and holding yourself back will not get you where you need to be any faster, if at all. Every one of the strokes and modalities that you need to learn can be learned. Go learn them.

Give it your all, and you will be hearing "that was the best massage I have ever had" more times than you can imagine.

"Do or do not. There is no try."

-Yoda, Jedi Master

4

THE DO'S AND DON'TS

Over the years, I have shared many intriguing conversations with my clients. For those who want to talk, the conversations more often than not lead somewhere that provides me with an opportunity to learn, or connect, or laugh. And laugh I have. There are times I thought my client would fall off the table. It is true that we should never be the ones to initiate conversation. But the times that it is encouraged by the client, it is so FUN. This is partly because I like people. I find them interesting. Partly because I work with such a wide, varied group of people that I feel I am constantly learning. My business would not have been as successful as it is without my clients' advice over the years. I might not have written this book, without many of them urging me to take my success to the next level. Most importantly, had I not listened to their needs, I would never have kept their business in the first place. I know you've heard over and over to listen to the client, not to place your beliefs in front of what the client is requesting from you. But I am afraid it must be repeated, given the complaints I have heard over the years. Many Massage Therapists simply aren't listening. You need to, or you could lose your dream client.

I have a client who is my dream client. We'll call him Rick. Rick made his first fortune by the age of thirty. At this time he was the neighbor of Bob Hope. As you may already know, Bob is a legend among LMTs because he received a massage EVERY DAY, for over thirty years. He swore that it would keep him alive until the age of 100. And it did, he lived to be a very healthy, vibrant 100 years old. Bob was also notorious for getting everyone he could around him to follow this same pattern. His friends in the rat pack, loved ones, and neighbors. Bob is no longer with us but, in Rick, his legend lives on. He too aims to get a massage every day. He probably hits the mark twenty-five days per month. He tips very, very generously. He buys massages for everyone he loves at this generous rate. He is kind, and warm, and funny. He is the ultimate dream client. He shared a story with me during our first massage session. And I listened. My listening is one of the things that made him trust me and want to call me back. His story went something like this: "I have many Massage Therapists around the world. I like to develop long-term relationships with them. In fact, one particular MT I have been working with for over thirty years.... So one day during a treatment, an MT that I had been seeing for about ten years was going on and on about how flower essences, and how scattering flowers on her friend, had saved her from dying of cancer. Now this wasn't the first bizarre thing she had said to me. She'd been getting weirder and weirder over the last two years. I usually just kept my mouth shut because I liked her. But this time I reminded her that I wasn't into this woo-woo stuff. And you know, she just kept going on about flowers and hocus pocus, and miracles... And I finally looked up at her and said "You and I have been working together for ten years. TEN YEARS. And now I want you to turn around, and walk out that door... and don't come back."

I have no problem admitting that I was more than a little intimidated by this man after hearing this story. But I wanted to be the replacement for that Massage Therapist. And I knew he was waiting for a response. So I gave him one. I laughed. I relayed a story about the time I was so determined that ear candles were bogus, and was so tired of hearing the opposite, that I burned one and then popped a chunk of the residual "ear wax" from the candle into my mouth to prove it. (Turns out I was right, it was just melted candle wax.) He cringed, and then laughed. He knew, in that moment, we were a good fit. Whether I believed in flower essences, ear candles or chanting to the full moon... he was never going to hear about it. Through my story, I had assured him of that. By listening, and responding accordingly, I landed my dream client.

Let's assume his previous Massage Therapist was earning, what I now make from him... she lost around $400,000 over the next ten years and a remarkable $1,200,000 over the next thirty years. All because she wasn't listening to his needs or desires. She was focusing on her own needs (i.e. beliefs). You may think his response was a little harsh. I look at it as a business transaction. He was losing A LOT of money in that hour while he was lying on her table. She was focused on herself. So focused, in fact, she refused to honor the request of her client, so that she could "share" her agenda. We have all made the mistake of saying too much, at one time or another. But I have learned to keep my opinions far from my clients. (Unless they BEG me to share them, and then I sugar coat everything with humor.) It is simply not worth losing one of them, and all the future clients they will send my way.

I have worked with a wide variety of clients over the last decade. In that time I have accumulated quite the list of Do's and Don'ts from their stories and admissions. Time and time again I have heard the same complaints about previous massage experiences. Some are shocking to me. Some, admittedly, I have to sometimes remind myself not to commit. You too will have days you are "off" and may have a difficult time focusing on your client's needs. Maybe you're tired. Perhaps you have an appointment scheduled right after and feel the urge to clock-watch. Whatever it may be... it is going to come up. It is a part of this industry. However, you are expected, and being paid, to be present for that client's needs the entire time they've hired you. So get used to it. Keep checking in with the client whenever you zone out. Take a deep breath when you don't feel like listening. Focus on your clients as if they are human beings with needs, and you are there to fulfill them. As Robert

Tisserand so eloquently put it, "Love what you do. Enjoy listening to people. It can be hard work, but the potential for helping people is tremendous."

I encourage you to follow this list of Do's and Don'ts. These are an accumulation of the expectations of the most respected and affluent clients in the world. This will ensure that you turn each new client into a devoted regular client.

DO: Accept credit cards.

If you want to be taken seriously as a business, work at hotels, or with VIPs and celebrities, you must accept credit cards. NO exceptions. Massage is a high-ticket item. It simply isn't fair to expect your client to find the time to withdraw cash for you. And it is very easy to set up a merchant account. The whole process has become very streamlined. You no longer even have to have equipment to process payment, you simply do it over any touch tone phone or your computer. (I chuckle inside every time I see an LMT struggle with a credit card imprint machine.) The process is easy. You simply respond to prompts over the phone. The purchase amount will be verified on the spot, you'll be given a confirmation number. You write out a quick receipt for you client, and you're done. The money will be directly deposited into your bank account within 48 hours. The best merchant card processing company that I have found in terms of efficiency, helpful staff and low monthly fee is Trans First www.transfirst.com. I have added a direct link from my website www.hundredthousanddollarmassage.com which will make the sign-up process easier for you.   It'll take just a few minutes of your time to set it up. Once you get use to using it, you'll wonder why you didn't always.

DON'T: Give a cookie cutter massage.

My number-one client complaint is this. MTs graduate from school with a signature massage memorized, and that is all they do. If there is a memorization of strokes or any other kind of repetition in your massage, you need to break out of that routine and get in touch with your client. Listen intently to what your client needs. If they express pain in an area, they want that area treated, and most likely more time spent on it. If you are following a routine they won't get what it is they need. Consider practicing on people who will provide brutally honest feedback with you. Take extended education classes if need be. If you do not break out of your rut, your business will never be as successful as you would like it to be.

DO: Continue giving your client 100% while they sleep.

If your client requests deep tissue massage, falls asleep for ten minutes, and wakes up to find you petting them... you've just lost a client. The benefits of the massage you are giving are present while the client is asleep, awake, and for days and weeks after the massage ends. Don't short them what they need because you are feeling lazy that day.

DON'T: Give your client energy work unless requested.

You may believe that a form of energy work is exactly what your client needs. But unless they have asked you for it, your good intentions may be completely misread. Consider that your energy work may be perceived as you being lazy, delusional, scary, disrespectful, time wasting, or snake oil selling. I am a Reiki Master and I NEVER give energy work where it is not requested. It is simply disrespectful of others' beliefs. You must always remember that your opinion of what others need is just that: YOUR opinion.

DO: Avoid medical diagnosing.

Despite the fact that it is illegal, I see LMTs do this quite often. Diagnosing may result in misdiagnosing, fear, or mistrust in other healthcare providers. There has been more than one occasion that I felt a client had been misdiagnosed and was prescribed the wrong treatment or surgery. In each of these scenarios I suggest that they get a second or third opinion. I always let them know that I was not qualified to diagnose them, but that I believe getting as many opinions before surgery is always a good idea.

DON'T: Be uninsured against liabilities

Clients want to know that you are what they define as "professional" this includes licensing and insurance. I'll spare you the horrific details about the client who tripped getting off my massage table and landed with his head in the wall. He fortunately accepted responsibility for the incident, and my insurance was never contacted. But the point is: freak accidents happen. Things you could never prepare for or expect. For around $199 a year you can get insured for $2,000,000.00 through International Massage Association at: www.imagroupinc.com. I also have provided a link for you on my site www.hundredthousandollarmassage.com.

DO: Avoid using oil unless requested.

You may have heard differently. But let me explain. Oil does not rinse off easily. Many people have allergic reactions to nut oils. Many more break out from the use of it. It requires a shampooing to remove it from the hair. It stains clothes. It stains sheets. After you dry your massage sheets with oil on them they will smell rancid. This becomes costly and inconvenient for both you and your client. I have been using Biotone's Advanced Therapy Massage Lotion for over ten years. It's hypoallergenic, easy to clean, fragrance free, and doesn't absorb into the skin too quickly, allowing your hands to remain in contact with the body more often. You can buy it at www.amazon.com.

Or link to it at www.hundredthousanddollarmassage.com. My clients often thank me for selecting a product with THEM in mind. Your clients will thank you for it too.

DON'T: Use scented products unless requested.

The same clients who appreciate lotion over oil need the lotion to be unscented. They are up and running to somewhere important after the massage, often business-related. The last thing they want is to smell to high heaven. Always allow your clients either the option of scented. Remember Pavlov's dogs? A scent that inspires a wonderful memory in you can bring up something upsetting for your client. On a side note: clients secretly feel it cheapens the experience if you charge them extra for scent. If you must, simply raise all your prices by $5 or so and have that make up the difference.

DO: Refer to your customers as clients, not patients.

According to a great many of my clients, being called a patient makes them feel as if you are calling them "sick". They don't appreciate it. The typical client gets a massage for a variety of reasons. One of the biggest reasons is to relax. The idea of seeing a doctor is not the least bit relaxing to most people. But this is the subconscious train of thought that goes through your client's mind when you call them a patient. Also, it creates expectations that you can provide medical care outside of your scope. It isn't appreciated by many Physical Therapists, Chiropractors, or Doctors, all with whom you should be networking.

DON'T: Massage the face after massaging the feet.

Okay, there is an exception to this. Keep a bottle of hand sanitizer with you and quickly sanitize your hands after working with the feet. Be sure to mention to the client that you have sanitized. Otherwise more of them than you would imagine simply aren't enjoying the rest of the massage as much as they could be. They're too busy thinking "yuck!" I do this because I prefer starting the client's face down so that their clogged sinuses can drain before the massage ends. And I like to end with a face/ neck/ scalp massage to really WOW them before the massage ends. Whichever way you prefer to start and end your sessions, don't gross them out by rubbing their feet all over their face. They'll be grateful, even if they don't say so.

DO: Offer a variety of music.

Quite frankly, many of the massage music CDs for sale are not the highest quality music. But music selection is important. It sets the mood. I have connected with celebrity clients through nothing more than selecting music for them I thought they would enjoy. This is an intuitive skill, similar to the intuition that guides your touch. Always let the client know before the massage begins that they can request a different CD if they don't love the first one. Expect higher tip percentages when you match the right music with the right client. Likewise, expect lower tips with music that grates their nerves or isn't appropriate (avoid heartbreak or battle scenes in movie soundtracks). Music enhances the entire massage experience, if chosen wisely. An innovative music collection was released in 2007 that receives rave reviews from my clients. The series is called ROCKABYE BABY! The Beatles, Led Zeppelin, Bob Marley, Smashing Pumpkins, Coldplay, and even Metallica songs have been recreated for children's bedtime. These tracks work wonderfully to calm and relax your clients while the familiar tunes put smiles on their faces. You can find the series at www.amazon.com. For your convenience, I will also be listing new music for you regularly in my blog at www.hundredthousandollarmassage.com and I will provide links to my personal selections.

DON'T: Initiate conversation.

I know you've heard this before, but it takes a lot of discipline to follow through. Your client may be the one initiating conversation, and you should, of course, politely respond without too much detail. Keep your answers short and succinct. Typically a client will begin with one of two questions to get you talking. "Where did you go to school for massage?" or "Where are you originally from?" are common opening questions. Usually they are feeling a little uncomfortable with the silence because they aren't used to it. Their minds haven't had time to disengage from work deadlines, relationship issues or to-do lists. So answer their questions respectfully, engage in full conversation in a relaxing tone if that is what you feel the client is truly wanting. However, about mid-way through the massage it's a good idea to clam up. I usually say, "I've been talking your ear off, let's make sure you get the last half of the massage in silence." Though they didn't know it was what they needed, they always thank me afterward. There are occasional exceptions to this rule. Some clients request to be talked to from beginning to end. They claim the chitchat relaxes them. Of course, we should give them what they want. The good news is these are typically the funniest clients you'll get to work with. So that one in a thousand is worth saving your voice box for!

DO: Leave them something to remember.

It goes without saying that you should make sure a client gets your business card. A receipt is a good idea too. So why not add a breath mint, chocolate, or bottled water to their list of goodies to take home? The expense is minimal and it will add value to the session in terms of warmth and caring outside of the actual treatment. Nice gestures don't go unnoticed or unremembered.

DON'T: Put cold hands on your client.

It is intensely jarring to have icy cold hands placed on your body when you are expecting nurturing touch. My hands are like little ovens, so luckily I don't have this problem. But for those of you that do, find a solution that works. Some options are to always wash your hands in hot water before each massage or on cold days slip a hand warmer into your pockets, and wrap one around your bottle of lotion. Microwave the lotion before the massage if you have access to a microwave, it will help keep the warmth in your hands. Always store your massage lotion in a warm place. Follow these simple tips and your clients will be warm and relaxed.

DO: Turn off your phone.

If for some reason you forget, apologize as if you accidentally just hit the client upside the head. You basically did. A cell phone ringing in the middle of the massage is totally counterproductive to the relaxing state your client is seeking and paying good money for. Encourage your clients to shut off their phones as well. Having said this, many of your clients these days can't get themselves to be away from their phone for an hour. They're worried about the kids, have a conference call, need to talk to their teammates about the game.... refrain from passing judgment and eagerly pass the phone to them when it rings. Many of them will express embarrassment. Gently assure them it's no problem at all. You are a professional, and nothing is going to break your concentration while giving them the best massage they've ever had.

DON'T: Assume that you know better than your client.

I hear this one too often. Many MTs simply refuse to give their client light Swedish massage when they request it, or Deep Tissue when they request that. I saw this first hand after I instructed a friend on how to give a massage to his girlfriend. By the end of training he had learned the basics and was giving a great amateur massage. Later in the week I met up with his girlfriend and she expressed dismay that he now wanted to massage her every day... very hard and deep... and in response to her protests he would say "this is good for you." She asked why I trained him in such a way. After explaining that I trained him to repeatedly check in with her comfort level and to never give more pressure than requested... the girlfriend and I had a good laugh together. It was then that I saw how it is that some people need to "know what is best for others." No matter how many times I had reminded him that he needed to listen to what his girlfriend wanted in terms of pressure, he had given her what he liked for himself. This story sounds atrocious to a Licensed Massage Therapist, an amateur burying his elbow into a protesting innocent girl's back is horrible, right? The reality is that Licensed Massage Therapists do just this every day. We lose potential lifelong clients because of it. More importantly, we lose valuable faith in our industry by the people who have chosen to go out on a limb and give us a try. We have enough odds stacked against us as healers and professionals, so let's not add to it by disrespecting our clients' physical needs and boundaries. Let us instead, elevate our profession's reputation through achieving impressive results; ones that are achieved by listening and responding to our clients' needs.

DO: Provide a massage studio that is professional, clean and

safe.

Clients notice every little detail of your massage space. While you can't please all of your clients with your choice of decor, there are a few simple rules to follow in setting up a space that will keep them coming back rather than running for the hills. Keep it clean. Each day wipe everything down and sweep the floor. Once a week do a deeper cleaning. This includes entryways and walkways up to the massage room. Keep your space separate from your living area. If your space is located in your house, have an outside door connected to it. This also makes it a very clear and undisputable tax write-off, which will benefit you greatly. Don't have visible garbage cans, children's toys, or other unsavory household reminders near the outdoor walk way to your business entry. In terms of setting up your space, keep it as simple as you can. Make sure the client can see the doorway from where the head of the table is placed. Keep colors in the room light and relaxing. Keep furniture all the same scale and style. Add extras that will be needed, such as a wastebasket, robe and slippers for bathroom trips, eye mask, cough drops, tissue, a small mirror for touching up, etc. Be sure to hide all these extras in a cupboard or armoire of some kind. Anything that isn't hidden away should be attractive with clean lines and no wires showing if you can help it. Think spa environment, not grandma's house. (Grandmas may be comforting to you, but creepy to someone else.) Floating shelves on the walls look amazing lined with candles in glass votives. I suggest white linens and sheets. They impart a clean feeling and can be bleached if stained. Waffle blankets and matching waffle robes can be found at: www.amazon.com. None of this need be expensive. In fact, if you keep the space clean and modern you'll be buying less and saving money. I suggest buying coordinating pieces from Modern Furniture www.modernfurniture.com or saving money on eBay www.ebay.com. (You can save a ton of money buying any of the products I mention in this book on eBay. Access their site, and all others mentioned from www.hundredthousanddollarmassage.com for one-stop shopping, direct links, and special offers.) Finally, hang a few hooks for your clients' clothes. Keep tall baskets under the massage table for sheet storage if you're in a small space. If you have a small massage room with low ceilings, hang white curtains from the ceiling to the floor on walls with windows to lengthen the ceiling height with one long clean line. Paint the walls an expansive color. Be sure to group similar items in clusters of odd numbers. Remember, organization is attractive. If you can first learn how to be organized, and locate anything in your massage room in ten seconds or less, your clients will feel more at peace there. Call it creating the energy of a room, Feng Shui, or whatever you want to call it; just do it. If you aren't design savvy and this is overwhelming to you, ask a friend to help in exchange for a few massages. You'll be amazed what many people will do for a massage or two.

DON'T: Change your phone number.

I have made this mistake and paid dearly for it. Your past clients will find a new LMT before they find you. It's fairly easy now to transfer phone numbers within regions. Cell phone numbers can be easily switched from one company to another. Find an easy-to-remember, professional-sounding number and stick with it. If you can get a number that spells out "massage" or something clever, that is always a bonus. Whatever you do, stick with that number. Your clients and referrals want to find you easily. This advice also covers business names, and basic logos.

DO: Keep your opinions to yourself.

Of course you know to avoid conversations about politics, religion, and war. But these days, it seems people get upset about the simplest topics. Don't fall into a trap of saying the wrong thing. I once had a client discussing a very heated political scenario with me. He and I had directly opposing opinions (although he didn't know it). It seemed as though my tight-lipped approach to the whole thing was upsetting him. He spoke with increasing vehemently about the subject until I finally said, "It was a great tragedy and caused such unnecessary pain for so many people." Why did I say this? Because it was a belief we both shared. When I offered this universal response he automatically assumed that I shared his viewpoint. He felt I understood his personal opinion of that suffering. I was able to hold onto what I believed while calming my client down and getting him to trust me so that we could get further into the business of relaxing him. Be smart. Find the angle that will appease, while you can still hold on to your personal truth. You'll keep your both your clients AND your conscience.

DON'T: Pass judgment on your clients.

This seems easy, I know. But it can be tough. Some of your clients are going to be difficult. People are people. They have imperfections. They may be on a path in life that you don't identify with or understand. They are right where they belong, and so are you. Maybe the worst example I ever heard of an MT failing miserably at non-judgment was this story: Sally went to receive her first massage. She was nervous, as is expected. Before session began the MT provided a health intake form, which she then filled out. After assessing the form the MT asked about Sally's profession. She replied that she worked at a coroner's office. She went on to explain that she cleans and prepares the dead for funerals. "I didn't want to lie," she adds to the story at this point. The MT responds that she may have to leave the massage halfway through to vomit and "purge any negative energy." Do I have to tell you that the client's experience was traumatic? That she was totally on edge the entire massage wondering if this MT was going to be ill from touching her? That she never received a massage again? This, of course, is an extreme example. But it exemplifies how we harshly many people judge one another on nothing more than personal belief systems. Whether this Massage Therapist believed that the dead are negative energy, the dead have no energy or that death is merely a part of life, she should have reined in her judgment before she spoke. She had an opportunity to provide acceptance to Sally about her misunderstood profession. That would have been the greatest gift of healing she could have given her. Don't miss every opportunity to give your clients what they need. Always remember that we heal people with more than just our touch.

DO: Be a clock-watcher.

It can be difficult in the beginning of this profession to get the timing of a massage down. But it's important. Just as you don't want to cut your client short of valuable massage time, likewise you cannot make your client late for their next meeting. Always treat each appointment with equal respect in terms of timing. You are not doing anyone any favors when you go over time by fifteen minutes, least of all yourself. In the very near future, you will be very busy and you will need to be structured and disciplined in how much time you allot for each one of your clients. If you genuinely feel that you may need more time with a client to fulfill their needs, ask if they would like to extend the massage for optimal results, or if not, what areas they would like to have "brushed over" so that you can focus on their main areas of complaints. Tip: Ask them about ten minutes into the massage, after you have found their sore spots, and they have an idea of your abilities. If they have the time, they'll say yes. Asking before they know the quality of massage they are getting, they will typically say "no" automatically.

DON'T: Be inconsistent with your policies.

If you need to have every new client sign an agreement of your policies to get you to reinforce them, do it. In fact, I recommend it. Inform the clients of your cancellation and no-show policies. If you accept payment from Labor and Industries (L & I), Personal Injury Protection (PIP), or Health Insurance, have a policy explaining whether or not the client will be responsible for payment in the case of under-payment by the companies, and if so, what percentage of the total bill the client is expected to pay. If your one-hour massage is actually a fifty-minute massage, with ten minutes used for paperwork, billing or table setup, let them know that too. This will help to clarify expectations for your clients, and will increase their trust in you as a professional. And most importantly, you'll have more than a leg to stand on when a client complains of any of your policies. After all, they signed off on them. Be smart. Protect yourself. Follow your policies to the letter.

DO: Practice non-invasive draping techniques.

This is a tough one for many new graduates. For nine months or a full year you were most likely graded on the wedgies you gave your client. If you didn't wrap your client in something that resembled an adult diaper, you failed. Now, entering the real world you are being told to unlearn all that practice? Yes. That is precisely what you are being told. And here's why: clients feel that you are inexperienced or uncomfortable with their body when you drape with techniques that require more than one step to achieve full coverage. This in turn, makes them feel uncomfortable. I know this seems counterintuitive to what you have learned. You were probably told that these types of draping techniques would make everyone feel safer. But stop and think about how much effort, limb moving, and accidental exposure happens with these techniques. I wish that I could explain to you how to drape more effectively in writing, but unfortunately I can't. However, I am creating a video on how to do just that. You can find it at: www.hundredthousanddollarmassage.com.

DON'T: Forget to keep the room void of distracting noises.

This includes squeaky tables, ticking clocks, popping and snapping gum (totally inappropriate), massage lotion pumping (use a flip top bottle), and bottles of massage lotion that have been allowed to get too empty that make loud sputtering noises as air mixes with lotion. All of these are very preventable. Maintain your equipment, sound-check the room before clients enter, and put a fountain in the room to absorb any additional noises. These small annoyances will leave a bad impression on the client even if they like your massage ability.

They may not know why they opt to find another LMT, but they usually will.

DO: Be on time.

When scheduling a client, as with anything else in business, over-deliver and under-promise. If you will be five minutes late for an appointment and you know it, set the appointment for fifteen minutes later. If your client insists on an appointment time and you may be late, provide them with fair warning. But do your absolute best to be on time. Do whatever it takes to have your table set up and your hands washed and your client relaxed and on the massage table no later than five minutes after the initially scheduled start time. This applies to all areas of business, but is especially important with massage. Your tardiness is unprofessional. You eating in the car, driving ten miles over the speed limit, worried about being late, and apologizing in a panicked state isn't relaxing for you or your client. So do your best to prepare and set up your day so that you will be early everywhere, and if something does detain you, just take a deep breath and know that it will be okay. You are a professional.

Stay relaxed and quickly apologize and let them know it won't happen again. No long stories, no drama. They'll forgive you unless it becomes a habit.

We are all human. Stuff happens. We are not perfect. Striving to be the very best we can be, and finding it within ourselves to immediately forgive ourselves of our imperfections is a necessary part of being a healer. Being professional and displaying discipline is important. Self-forgiveness and self-compassion are everything. You must have these traits yourself to be able to give them to your clients day in and day out. Seek balance in all that you do. And most importantly, listen to, and honor, the needs of your clients. This will build the clientele of YOUR dreams.

"What a strange power there is in clothing."

- Isaac Bashevis Singer

5

DRESS FOR SUCCESS

How you present yourself to the world through your personal image is the first thing people see and the last thing people remember of you. We live in a society where first impressions are crucial. Perhaps you have been led to believe that appearances do not matter when you are a healer. Or have been encouraged to believe your business will be successful without worrying about such trivial things. If so, you've been led astray. No matter how evolved we become as a culture, human beings are still biologically driven to judge appearances. No one will change this in our lifetime. Trying to will only keep one flat broke. I am not merely suggesting that despite your amazing hands-on abilities, being unkempt will limit your success. I am insisting it.

There was a time, in the 1980s and before, when massage was a niche market. Talented Massage Therapists were often self-taught, and were able to charge whatever they deemed appropriate for their demographic: clientele, number of years practicing, etc. There weren't many competitors, and few such luxuries were offered to the public, so there were a limited number of choices. Massage Therapists working from a studio or their homes were considered artists and healers, and it was acceptable for them to be a little outwardly eccentric in their appearance. On the flip side, there were Massage Therapists working at the fanciest and most prestigious of hotels, spas, and in celebrity homes, generally wearing the typical massage uniform: khakis, white polo, and white sneakers. I personally know of an LMT who wore this bland uniform until the day he was "retired". In the beginning of his career in the 1980s he earned $80,000 a year. That was A LOT of money back then. By the time he retired his income was under $20,000 per year, and his pride had wilted. In twenty years he had gone from the top of his game to the very bottom, simply because he was unwilling to take a look around him and accept how the world of massage was changing.

The profession that you have chosen has now entered a new day. There are so many opportunities available to you. All thanks to those few Massage Therapists who started this health profession awareness. They were the brave pioneers, and they got to wear whatever they liked. But these days, with as many opportunities as are available to you, there are thousands of Massage Therapists looking to fill those same positions. You need to be prepared. You need to be noticed by the affluent. These are the ones who will refer you business, will be your regular clients, and will lease you that space in their building downtown. You need to be remembered. You will do this by being the best-dressed LMT they have ever laid eyes on.

I understand that you may not have had the best examples for this. Do not look to your MT friends for guidance. Chances are they are not as successful as you would like to be. Ditto your fellow Massage Therapy students. Ditto many of your massage instructors, for that matter. Look outside your profession to how the most successful people you know dress. Then consider any practical needs your clothing must meet. Now merge the two. Do you think Oprah would've made it where she is today without putting her best foot forward? After she landed that first radio job, she easily could have come to work in sweat suits every day. It would've been a heck of a lot more comfy than heels and fitted dresses. But Oprah had a future on her mind. She had a grand life to create. And she, like all other highly successful women, knows that looking successful creates success. Play the part and you will become it.

Admittedly, you do have a few restrictions in your choice of clothing to be able to do your job effectively. Your clothing should allow for movement and should not be too revealing. The material should be washable. Your shoes should be comfortable and flat-heeled. Imagine how many amazing things there are to wear that fill those four requirements. Why waste your image, possibly your best marketing tool, on clothes that get you unnoticed, and lose you potential clients? The people who are your best referrals and clients are used to quality: quality cars, quality products, and quality service. They see poorly constructed clothing from a mile away. You don't have to spend a million dollars to look like it. But you do have to place some importance on your image, until it becomes second nature.

I know that fashion may not be your forte. Worry-not. It is one of mine. And I am here to help. But first I need you to assume that your style can use some tweaking. If you haven't yet become a huge success, chances are you have been putting your money into traditional marketing and learning new massage techniques, both of which are also important keys to success. It may be difficult to find the money to invest in your wardrobe, but you must. It is a marketing expense, arguably, the most important one. Secondly, I'd like you to ask yourself "what am I going to lose by cleaning up, and making my image more professional? What could I possibly gain?" This may sting a little. But I really wish somebody had given me a little tough love on this subject years ago. It would have saved so much time! Once you are making $100,000 for three years straight, then you can decide to go back to your old image.

But I bet you won't want to.

Thanks to television programming, you can watch and learn with shows such as "What not to wear" and "Queer eye for the straight guy". These kind and fashionable souls have even put books out on the subject of dressing for your body type. This information is everywhere, if only you look. Bet you can find it at www.amazon.com (where you can also find this book). The day that

I walked into a massage with the most fashion savvy member of "Queer Eye"... only to see his eyes light up, and say "Wow. Look at you, Diva! You are not at all what I expected, you look fabulous!" I knew that I must be doing something right. Because of how I initially projected myself, he felt comfortable with me and on equal footing with me. This enhanced level of trust translated to a greater trust in my abilities as a Massage Therapist. Coincidentally, this added one more celebrity client to my regular client list. This, of course, is always a good thing.

Ask yourself, what did this client mean when he said, "You're not at all what I expected?" Do you want to be a Massage Therapist whose presence generates little enthusiasm, little trust, and, sadly, little respect? No, you don't. Many clients over the years have revealed that our appearance does indeed matter. It took me a very long time to grasp this concept. I would argue, "Why does it matter what I look like? I am a great Massage Therapist!" But as my appearance cleaned up for personal reasons, I saw the impact it made on my professional life and I had my "aha!" moment. If you dress on the level of your clientele, you are a reflection on them.

You become someone they could be friends with, see eye to eye with, and talk shop with.

Most Massage Therapists separate themselves from their most important clients by putting out an image that the client does not relate to. Thus, they limit the number of experiences and bits of information that would be provided to them otherwise. The connections you make based even partially on your new image will give you an advantage that is far-reaching. Trust me. I have been backstage at concerts, attended celebrity dinners, and socialized on mega-yachts. None of it would have happened if I had walked through the door in scrubs.

Michael Korda once claimed "The fastest way to succeed is to look like you're playing by other people's rules, while quietly playing by your own." Throughout the chapters of this book I will reveal many ways in which I believe this is sound advice, although what you wear may be arguably one of the most important ways. So let us begin shaping the outside of you to showcase the uniqueness of the professional you.

You have a unique look and presence. Accent that. Take the things about your style that you currently love, not the things you are dependent on, or hold on to for fear's sake... and ask how you can "grow it up" a bit. I am a huge believer in shopping on eBay www.ebay.com. There is nothing wrong with trying on clothes at the local department store or boutique, recording the designer, style name, color, sku number, and size and then hunting it down for a lot less money. In fact, once you find a favorite designer, you will learn that designer's sizing, and won't have to try things on any more.

A few years ago, I discovered a designer for women based out of Los Angeles named Rachel Pally. She was a dancer and decided to create a fashion line that was fluid and comfortable like dance clothes, but that could be worn in any situation. The result, I think, is nothing short of fabulous. And many celebrities agree. Last year, Rachel Pally's gaucho pants hit Oprah's "favorite things" list. Truthfully, I'm surprised it took her so long to figure out how fabulous her stuff is. She's been my best-kept secret for years. Rachel Pally's line can go from giving a massage, to yoga class, then out to dinner by quickly slipping on a chunky necklace and heels.

Her clothes appear refined yet casual. They provide unrestricted movement and accent a woman's shape without being showy or revealing. The pieces can be wrapped and folded into three or more different shapes, and her clothes never shrink or fade. Also, if something is too long for you... simply cut it off at the bottom. Amazing. You can find her line for sale at www.shopbop.com. I have provided a direct link to her line at www.hundredthousanddollarmassage.com.

Ladies, consider mixing her pieces with a quality scarf or pair of flats that you got for 30 -70% off retail price on eBay. www.ebay.com. If you wait and buy off-season and online, the stuff drops through the floor in price, and there is a much broader selection than on the sales rack at the local mall. If you're scared to buy online, I understand, but get over it. Have somebody who understands eBay, feedback, and PayPal, explain it all to you. It's a must. You will save bundles of money, even if you have one or two less-than-perfect experiences.

I know that money may be tight for you in the beginning. So start small. Mix and match five tops, three pairs of pants, and two pairs of flats. (You'll already be doing laundry, what is one more load?) I recommend both the pants and one pair of shoes is black for an urban / spa / professional look. Top your outfits with a yoga trench coat that you bought on eBay, and a large solid-color hobo bag to carry your massage supplies from Zappos www.zappos.com.

For both male and female MTs I adore the line of clothing by James Perse. What looks like an ordinary linen shirt, cotton tee, or sundress is in actuality the most comfortable and well-fitted garment you will possibly ever own, without being too revealing or restrictive. The men's pieces from this line embody a relaxed, professional, laid back style that I feel all MTs would benefit from projecting. The woman's line is great for basics to mix and match with Rachel Pally's line, but often lacks a striking color palette on it's own. James Perse for men is found at revolveclothing.com and the woman's line is also found there and shopbop.com.

Stay away from crazy prints and colors. Learn what colors look good on you. Learn to mix and match your clothes. Buy higher quality instead of high quantity, low quality choices. Never say, "It's too nice / expensive to wear for massage." If it fits the requirements, wear it. You can get any oil stains out with my favorite miracle stain remover "Washout", which you can buy at www.caycecures.com. (Direct link it from my site.) For ANY oil stain on your clothes of any kind, squeeze this extract from coconut oil on the spot (yes, it's scary the first time you do it) and wash it as usual. Inspect it before you dry it. Repeat the process until the spot is fully gone. Then dry or hang dry. Voila! No more oil stain. I cannot express how important quality is. It doesn't have to be designer labels, but it must be quality. In fact, stay away from designer names in visible places, or any other blatant advertising. Just keep yourself looking, simple and clean. This will allow for your unique presence and abilities to shine that much more.

And finally, professionals do not wear Birkenstocks, Uggs, sneakers, sandals, flip-flops, crocs, slippers or bare feet to work. Why would you? Close-toed flats are what's what for the busy professional female Massage Therapist. Cushy inserts are a must. Just remember to wear footies designed for flats, or your feet will smell atrocious! If the typical ballet flats feel a bit too girly for you ladies, there is a pair that has a square toe, or is in a fabric that suits you. Remember, until you define your style, the simpler the better. Again, be able to mix and match. Look for something that you can wear with your pants, Capri pants, or gauchos (never wear shorts!) and something you can slip off when the need arises. Make sure the bottoms have grip, or add your own. You don't want to be slipping and sliding while giving Deep Tissue to an NFL player. You'll need all the grounding and momentum you can get. Check out each season's flats at www.zappos.com. And men, don't be shy about upping the professional quotient of your shoes. It has been rumored for centuries that men are judged by the quality of their shoes. Don't get stuck in the white tennis shoes rut. If you don't have the money to buy a great pair of Italian shoes at first, check out Toms Shoes at revolveclothing.com. They are under $50, comfortable, and fashionable. Pair them with some James Perse slacks and linen shirt with the sleeves cuffed during massage and you're set to go. You are almost done. No good outfit is complete without great hair. Get a haircut: a current one. Do not let your mom, a friend, or your mom's friend cut your hair. Ladies, ask every woman you run into on the street who has a great haircut which stylist she sees. Who cares if she gives you a funny look? You will likely never see her again, and if you do... you will look fabulous. Tell your stylist that you need a cut that will look great in twenty minutes or less, because we MTs usually don't like to primp, and we need to be on our toes for those VIP clients. And contrary to what you may have heard... a good stylist really does like it when you bring in photos. The stylist should be able to tell you whether a style will work best for your facial structure and your time restraints. I have been taking less than ten minutes to fix my hair for ten years. Any one looking at me would say I have a fashionable look. Why? I spend money on my cut. Good cut = good grow out = fewer cuts at the end of the year = more money and time to live and work and play. Oh, and ladies, tweeze, wax or bleach any facial hair. The hair on your head being neglected is not so good. The hair on your face being neglected is disastrous. This goes for ear and nose hair too, gentlemen!

In fact, neglect of any basic hygiene and self-care necessities is a fast track to a business that fails. It is not my intention to offend anyone with the truth, but according to the many clients I interviewed, it is necessary to say it. For them, many

Massage Therapists are not up to basic standards of grooming, much less standards that will bring them a six-figure income. Most of you will find something interesting or funny or enlightening in what I am about to say. It is not my intention to offend anyone, only to encourage all of us to be the best we can be. So now let's talk about what's under your clothes...

Stay fit. Maintain a healthy weight. It is not uncommon for Massage Therapists to put on excess weight after a few years in the profession. Business picks up, the schedule is full, and a cup of coffee and a pastry replaces a well-balanced meal. You scoff now, but it has happened to the best of us. In a profession with a high rate of last-minute appointments, it requires a lot of diligence and foresight to provide your body with proper nutrition. I keep extra bottled water in my car and packages of organic nuts at all times. That way I always have a healthy and satisfying snack. When I didn't, I was fifteen pounds heavier. Don't let it happen to you. Keep the weight from coming on. Taking those extra pounds off later is so much more difficult than prevention ever is. I'm a firm believer in a junk-free diet that is high in fish and dark, leafy greens and nuts, and low in starches; and one that emphasizes organic, free range, and locally grown foods. Try to keep sugar and caffeine intake to a minimum.

I also suggest enrolling at your local YMCA (www.ymca.com) for your daily requirement of physical exercise. They have sliding fee scales when needed, free classes, two free personal training appointments and are very community-minded. You staying fit not only provides you with the energy needed to massage for years to come, and keeps you looking great, it is a great example for your clients to take care of their own bodies.

Stay clean. Use lightly scented or unscented products. I suggest going natural and/ or organic. You can find out exactly how toxic nearly any beauty product is at: www.skindeep.com or direct link it from my web site. There is a plethora of great product lines available to you in health food marketplaces, organic co-ops, and many big name grocery and drug store chains are carrying some of these product lines. So even if you live in an area that is not yet savvy to natural products, you have no excuses. I am so impressed with the products and philosophies of the Miessence product line that I have begun offering it for sale to my clients. It is the ONLY comprehensive product line that is certified to organic food standards in the world. You can buy products from me personally, either from a link to my umiesssentialorganics.com website through the HTDM web site or from any knowledgeable Miessence representative at www.miessence.com. And for inexpensive lotions, soaps, balms, and naturally scented massage oils I am smitten with a small company based out of Orcas Island in Washington called Island Thyme: www.islandthyme.com. You simply must try the rose rejuvenation face cream. Once you get used to natural fragrances you will be appalled at how truly toxic the average person smells every day. All those chemicals are not the least bit good for you. The essential oils in natural products do wonders for the body and mind. However, if you overload yourself in too much fragrance, natural or otherwise, you are offending people. And offending people is not good for business.

While we are on the topic of offensive odors: I have found that most natural deodorants do not work for me. They do not work for many people. Your body odor may seem okay to you. It may be great for your partner. Do not mistake it for being okay for everyone. If you insist on avoiding anti-perspirant deodorant, make sure that your armpit area is cleaned with baby wipes or soap and water before and after every massage, and also periodically throughout the day. Your personal choices in hygiene should not be forced upon your clients. They will notice. Remember the man I was telling you about who went from $80K a year to less than $20K? He repeatedly received complaints about his body odor. He chose to do nothing about it. As a result his client base died down to new clients only. If they came back, they requested someone else. What a shame. Can you believe wearing deodorant can mean a difference of $60,000 a year in your income? It's sad, but true.

And yet another thing that stinks: cigarette smoking. It is a horrible habit that will repulse any client that gets near you. You can't smell yourself, but your client can. Your breath smells like a dirty ashtray. Your sweat smells like nicotine. Your fingers are permanently yellowed. Don't think a shower will make it go away. After you quit and you massage people who smoke, you will understand everything that I am saying to you right now. You have two options as far as I can see: smoke, or be a successful Massage Therapist. You can't do both. It simply is not possible. If you chose to keep smoking, all the secrets in the world cannot help you build a strong business.

Another hygiene issue that keeps the clients away is unkempt hands and nails. Cut and file your fingernails. Often. If I paint mine, it is always a natural looking French manicure. Otherwise, just use clear polish. Your clients do not want to wonder what is lurking under those fingernails. And they certainly do not want to endure being scratched and poked throughout the treatment session. I never noticed other Massage Therapists' nails until a referring professional commented how much he appreciated my French manicures since, "most Massage Therapists have such manly, unkempt hands." Well, I was shocked. I had been getting a manicure only twice a month and was often embarrassed at the edges chipping away. Once I started to look around, I realized I was way ahead of the standard. Most Massage Therapists don't give their hands, the thing their new clients inspect most a second thought.

And finally, I have to bring up a couple of issues that may be a sensitive topic: bad breath and acne. I know these are embarrassing and complicated problems to have. But to be successful as a Massage Therapist, in the long run you must find a resolution to both of these issues. Commonly these problems are caused by food allergies. Discover what foods you are allergic to and omit them from your life. Seek instruction from professionals regarding these problems. A quick visit to the dentist or dermatologist may end your struggle. Sadly, I have witnessed very talented Licensed Massage Therapists not get hired or struggle to build a clientele because of either of these issues. I once struggled with acne in my early twenties after being blemish-free all through puberty. I understand how it can affect your self-esteem. How it feels to have people assume that it's lack of good hygiene that is creating the problem, even though you wash your face multiple times a day. I know you may not want to talk about it with anyone, but I am telling you that you must. It is necessary for you to achieve greater success.

Bottom line: if you want your odds of success to increase, you must not be offensive to the masses. I have a large tattoo on my back. My clients don't know it. Nor do any of the professionals that refer to me. Even in a liberal city like Seattle, discretion makes all the difference. Body art and piercing still make many people uncomfortable, and can express parts of an MT's personality with which clients may not feel safe. The same goes for body hair. Most North Americans are not ready for professional women with hairy legs and underarms, or men with purple goatees. You are a healthcare provider. Imagine if your first appointment with a psychiatrist or M.D. was with a woman covered in body art, twenty facial piercings, and visible rainbow-colored underarm hair; you might have some reservations. This is, of course, an extreme example, but it does exemplify how some clients will feel towards your smaller offenses.

Likewise, don't expose your armpits, have bare feet, or wear open-toed sandals. Some men find feet more sexually exciting than breasts. You wouldn't go into a massage with your top off, so don't go into one with your shoes off. Similarly, a client once complained to me about having to look at white athletic socks during a massage with another Massage Therapist many years before. Clients take note of such offenses and never forget. And they will never tell you. But they may end up telling others, killing your potential for new clients.

Does how you look have anything to do with how great you are as a Massage Therapist? No. Is it fair that people judge you on your appearance first and your abilities second? No, probably not. But it IS the reality. I don't want a door to get slammed in your face because of something silly, like what you are wearing. I want you to have every door flung wide open for you on your journey to success. Dressing with confidence and flair will only make it that much easier for you. I know a Massage Therapist who gets the first call from a high-end hotel, and as a result, books the highest number of massages there because of her appearance. Despite other Licensed Massage Therapists having higher customer satisfaction, and despite her low numbers of repeat clientele, she gets the work. I myself have turned away Massage Therapists interviewing for me because their image was not up to par. Don't let this happen to you. Walk through every door with your head held high. Be your best, brightest, and most beautiful self. Go get 'em, tiger!

"Doing business without advertising is like winking at a girl in the dark. You know what you are doing, but nobody else does."

\- Steuart Henderson Britt

6

ADVERTISING ON A SHOESTRING

Emma Harrison once said there are three things that you should spend your time doing: marketing, marketing, marketing. And the best way to do that is to have a memorable, attractive and confidence-inspiring image. Perhaps you are ready to begin choosing an image for your advertisements and media, or you may realize it is time to revamp your current image. Either way, you have the same basic principles to follow. I will be giving you the information that has helped me most in this area. I have provided you with marketing strategies that specifically apply to the unique business of Massage Therapy. However, there are plenty of great marketing books out there that will provide a broader overview of this topic. I am a big believer in research. The knowledge that I have gathered has been through reading and absorbing many different types of business books, manuals, and observing the behavior patterns of successful Licensed Massage Therapists. It also took me plenty of trial and error, which can be costly until you get it right. I am providing you with what I know works, and will give you an edge on your competitors, but that does not mean that there are not plenty of creative ideas that you can implement into your business image with help from other resources. Use every tool that is available to you. Make the growth of your company a fun and rewarding endeavor. After all, the more prosperous you are, the less you will worry, which ultimately means you will be able to give more where it counts: to your clients.

One of the unfortunate mistakes that I see many Massage Therapists make with their business image is the same that I see them make with their personal image. There are many Massage Therapists who are afraid to venture out of what their fellow Massage Therapists are doing. But the irony of this is that the average person in this profession is making less than the average cost of living. Therefore, by following their lead, Massage Therapists are essentially setting themselves up for poverty. This lean towards a more conservative marketing plan is justified some ways: you have to be careful in this industry to put out an image that isn't mistaken for a less "professional" business. And no one wants to spend money they don't have to try multiple images over the years. It's a waste to do so. And clients lose track of you when you make multiple changes to your marketing materials. I understand because of its finality, it is difficult to make permanent decisions for your company. I mulled over the name Umi for a year before I finally decided on it. While the name was one that could evolve with the growth of my company, I look back and wish that I been brave enough to commit to it much sooner.

By explaining why I chose my particular business name I can provide you with important considerations for choosing your own. First, I researched the massage businesses in my area that were successful. I felt that anything with the word "hands" in the title was over-used. I imagined a client flipping through the phone book saying to themselves, "Was it Healing Hands or Hands on Massage or...?" and I decided to avoid this scenario. It may be a different over-used word or phrase in your area, but there is at least one. Avoid it. You don't want to be confused with your competitors. Secondly, I wanted to have a name with versatility. Umi is Japanese for "sea" which can work with any of the current Zen-like, modern spa themes. It connotes a relaxing, Eastern, non-intimidating sound when spoken "ooh me" and is unusual enough that the chic-elite love it too. I thought "Umi Essentials" would be a fantastic name for a line of products, also. But wait, I hadn't had even a small clientele yet, so my name really should have the word "massage" in it. Otherwise, how would people know what Umi was?

I had this vision of working with primarily urbanites downtown, and acquiring occasional seated massage events in downtown businesses, so I came up with a version of the name where Umi was the acronym that it would eventually phase into. My initial image was under the moniker "Urban Massage." This version of the name has a much more business ring to the ears. Seattle is full of very left-brained individuals, many of them working in super-technical environments. Urban Massage's ads attracted these clients and brought more than a few seated massage events my way. The great thing is that I swapped back and forth between the names if one was more suitable than the other. I put out two entirely separate advertisements: Umi for the Swedish massage/spa clients and Urban

Massage for the business execs and company events. And it worked. Both names brought me in different groups of clients very effectively. Which brings me to this point: you may have more than one advertisement out on the market. And often it behooves you to do just that. It is not typically expensive to license two or more business names each year, and it can be a very clever way of attracting more clientele than one ad could ever do alone.

Once you've decided on a name (or two), it's time to get down to the business of choosing font types, creating a logo, catch-phrases and content, while taking your desired client base (demographic) into account to design an appealing business card. If all of this seems a little daunting, you're not alone. It takes practice, and an understanding of advertising that you may not have yet. However, if you are not able to come up with a marketing plan and outline before you graduate from school, be sure to design a suitable card with your name, a telephone number that will always stay with you (a cell phone), and any other basic information you may need to provide a potential client. Don't be caught empty handed... your initial card doesn't have to be perfect. But you do have to have one.

If you are able to pay a design professional to create your business card, you are fortunate. For the rest of you... barter, trade, beg and plead, if necessary. I did, and I'd do it again. I highly recommend being a part of the process and checking in with your designer periodically. Make sure you share the same vision as the project evolves. Many times you think you are on the same page with your designer and when you take a look at the final product, you realize that you both have to head back to the drawing board. This wastes precious time and money. It's much easier on the pocket book if you catch these differences along the way. Or, you can skip this process all together and get cool inexpensive cards made at www.moo.com.

When it comes to choosing a font, you first need to define what feeling you are trying to evoke with your ad. Brainstorm keywords that come to mind when you think of the image that you would like people assume is YOU through your ad. Those words may be "relaxing", "calm", "caring", "professional", "clean", "Zen", "reputable", "respectable", "responsible", "warm", or many others. There is a font out there somewhere that conjures up these emotions (even if only on a deep subconscious level). Find it. Search Healing Centers, Massage Therapists, Naturopaths, etc. on Google. Bring your examples to your designer, they should be able to guide you to the perfect font with the information you provided.

Font choice is important. Barbara Corcoran, a real estate mogul, claims that her first business card was a very simple card on high quality paper. The font she chose was the same font as Tiffany's, the world's most upscale jewelry seller. She already clearly understood the intense associations that people can draw when they see a particular font. She wanted her clients and future clients to see her as the best in the world. Hence, she "borrowed" Tiffany's font.

I encountered this type of powerful association first hand when I allowed the Yellow Pages to create an ad for me. Although I let them know which fonts I would like to use, and drew out an exact replica of what I wanted, it came back an absolute mess. My instructions were disregarded, and worse, the font looked like something out of a horror film. It was anything BUT Zen. Every time I looked at the ad, I got a sick feeling to my stomach. Who knows how the ad made my potential customers feel? I'll never know. I wasn't able to ask, as I didn't get a single call from it.

Which reminds me to impress upon you: NEVER let anyone design an ad for you that does not provide you the option of overseeing the design process. Hopefully you won't choose to advertise in a money pit such as your local telephone book, with all the advertising tidbits that I will be giving you, but if you must... design the ad first. Yes, it will cost you additional money, but it is so worth it. The web designers working for these types of companies have very little advertising knowledge or design savvy, in my experience. In fact, they always tried to guide me to make my ads look more like the other ads, which would have decreased the amount of business I attracted. They wanted me to have full-color, and more information, and no white space. Part of it was they trying to be helpful in a misguided way, most of it was just the sales staff trying to up-sell without concern for my income in the coming year. Take control of your "baby" or allow someone you trust to do just that. The ad "experts" working for these companies are generally straight out of a two-year design program making ten bucks an hour.

Don't let their well meaning, but misguided intentions cost you thousands of dollars.

The ad that brought me the highest response rate was one I designed myself. It brought me events from the ballet, major department stores, restaurants, wineries and many executives. The ad was ridiculously simple: the name, three colors, white background, aqua logo and black typeface, a thick black outline around the ad, lots of white space, a small list of services offered, an eye catching one-line phrase "At your door in an hour," a minimal outline of the Seattle skyline at the bottom and credit card logos at the bottom. It was a very clean, modern, and professional image. When viewing a page of massage ads with curly or unconventional fonts, covered in typeface, full-color pictures, and double boxing around the ads, most with yellow background, the only ad that POPPED was mine. It stuck out from the rest like a glowing beacon of light. While everyone else was trying to out-do each other with information, they forgot a basic of good image making: how to pull the buyers' eyes to your ad before they think to look at any others. If you can catch their first glance, they are more likely to call you first, even if they study the ads of others. It is initial attraction that sells your ad over 80% of the time. Once a potential new client's attention was caught, they were pulled in by my offering something no one else was offering... super-fast service. And I aimed to make that a statement a reality 100% of the time. I only missed the mark twice in three years. Which brings me to my last point about ad content: make sure you do not over-promise. Under promising and over-delivering is the way to turn initial clients into long-term clients.

The second reason why my ad not only drew in, but captured, my audience with the phrase "At your door in one hour" is that this phrase embodied a key marketing tactic that is commonly underutilized by Massage Therapists. A high percentage of successful advertisements draw consumers in to purchasing their product by engaging them subconsciously. They do this by asking the potential customer a question that derives an automatic, albeit subconscious, agreement or affirmation. By saying "at your door in one hour." I was answering the client's most common first asked question. Their subconscious train of thought was to feel connected to the ad. "Wow, this "Umi" already understands my impossible work schedule, this company must be filled with understanding, accommodating Massage Therapists. I'm in. Where do I sign? Yes. Yes. Yes." You get the point. You've seen less subtle question - based advertisements for injury lawyers: HAVE YOU BEEN IN AN ACCIDENT AND NEED A GOOD LAWYER? YOU MAY BE ELIGIBLE TO SETTLE FOR $1,000,000! Again, you get my point. The truth is, depending on the market you are advertising to, this type of headline (though perhaps a bit more subtle) can increase your odds of turning that looky-lou into a client who has made the phone call and scheduled a first appointment. This type of advertisement is particularly good for educating people who are not aware of their medical coverage benefits, worker's compensation benefits, or Personal Injury Protection Claims. There are a lot of injured people in the world who haven't a clue that massage can help heal them, reduce their stress, or decrease risk of injury. There are even more who don't understand that when they are injured on the job, or in an auto accident that their massage bill may be partially or fully paid by insurance. If they did, a whole lot more massage clients would exist in the world. A side benefits of advertisements that ask questions, is that you can also supply the answer. The answer can be packed full of statistical findings presented in a fun and easy-to-read format. This is a great way to build trust, generate interest, educate and inspire new clients. For example:

> ## Holidays have you stressed?
> ### Give yourself the gift of massage.
> ### We're only a call away.
> ### (206) 555-1212

Every type of business in the world advertises this way. Let's jump aboard. Effective advertising is consistently effective across many markets. Always research what works for the particular demographic you are marketing to. Consider what that group of clients first question would be if you were to answer a call from them, and beat them to the punch line by answering it in your advertisements. You'll be amazed how effective this form of marketing is. Another great way to increase credibility with clients is to have a website built. It will give your image a boost all by itself. You can get away with a web presence of only one page at first. Just put your logo, business name, eye-catching design, list of services, location, hours of operation, payment types accepted, contact information, and perhaps a company statement or belief, or a quote that sums up your beliefs succinctly. There are an amazing number of great quotes to find at: www.quotegarden.com. Search the web for sites that you like, and create a list of them with reasons why you like that particular site. Maybe it's the colors of one, the usability of another, the logo on yet another. Bring all this information to your web designer. Have him or her build your site so that if you later choose to add pages it's easy to do. To make this an even more streamline process for you, I will be adding a web page builder on to www.hundredthousanddollarmassage.com. I'll make it very easy for you to design a beautiful and comprehensive site that showcases your massage business very effectively. This should save you time and money over using a web designer.

In this current age, all products and services are moving their advertising presence to the web. Keyword searches have now made attracting the right audience very easy. You can research effective keywords at www.googlekeywords.com. It is no longer acceptable for only 10% of Massage Therapists to have a website. We need to embody the same standards of marketing as other professionals. There are other easy ways to advertise on the web quickly too. Facebook now rivals any country in terms of population. Placing a compelling ad in the side bar of your demographic can be a cost effective way to advertise to local niche markets. The great thing is that the cost per click options mean that you will only pay for actual traffic, unlike paper advertisers who will charge you regardless of performance. Don't fall behind on this trend. Just as a cell-phone is a must have in this business, so is a computer and high-speed internet service, a web site. Don't even think of dealing with dial-up, it is too slow to do you any good at all. You will lose more time than it's worth to save a few bucks with dial-up. If you aren't yet computer savvy, don't be scared to learn. I once was. I refused to give in to the idea of having technology in my life. I still choose my battles. I don't have television. I try to use my cell phone for business only. But the truth is, without cell phone service and high-speed internet, I would still be flat broke.

Whether you are advertising with paper materials or on the web, photos are always a good idea. Have a photographer take a professional head shot of you in black and white. Impress upon them that the photo should be very professional. More often than not, Massage Therapists with a photo of themselves on their ads gets the client. It creates a sense of trust with new clients that words alone cannot convey. Similarly, photos for your advertisements can be purchased from stock photography websites. This saves you the time and money of hiring a photographer. There are occasionally good photos that will fit your theme that you can download for free. Give www.fotosearch.com a try for free photos. However, be careful with ad color. Depending on what printer you go to for paper advertisements, or what monitor a client is looking at your ad colors can vary greatly. The last thing you want is a photo advertisement that represents you as having a green face.

Besides paper and web advertising, there is a plethora of creative advertising ideas that require little to no money, but a bit more courage and creativity. I know of one very successful Chiropractor who began advertising by passing his cards out in his business while wearing a t-shirt that said "Ask me about Chiropractic," and carrying a model of a human spine. He elevated to great success in just five years. His empire began with a little creativity, a very small budget, and a lot of courage. Likewise, I know of one LMT put advertisements on both sides of her purple Cruiser PT and daily circled the lake in her area of business. As a result of the exposure this created, her business grew rapidly in the first year. While these examples may seem courageous, the fact is that these types of advertising are effective. They capture attention. This gets people asking about you and talking to you. Once they are talking to you, it puts you in the advantageous position of educating them on your services. And finally, it creates repetitive recognition in people's minds. Each and every time locals saw that purple car, the Massage Therapist inside of the vehicle became more familiar. Brilliant. Everyone will tell you to drop cards off everywhere, which a good idea. But to be one step ahead of the competition you need to inspire curiosity in people. People are busy. They are inundated with stimuli every day. Figure out how you are going to snag their attention, and do it. Don't look back. Don't worry about looking silly. Remember: It has always been the individuals who dare to think outside the box that become the most successful and, ultimately, the most inspiring to others.

Speaking of inspiring others, your most creative, brilliantly executed advertisements won't only be recognized by new clients. They will grab the attention of competitors as well. And if your competitors' businesses aren't as successful as yours, often they will steal part of your marketing campaign. Often they will steal a scarily large portion of it. There really is little that you can do about this. It is the nature of business. You, at some point, will unknowingly "borrow" ad content from an advertisement that caught your fancy years before and remained in your subconscious. I'm not trying to defend plagiarism. I'm just trying to get you to understand that this happens to all of us at some point or another, and being at the top of your game requires constant evolution. You won't stay at the top of any profession by sitting back on what works. Others follow your lead and easily pass you by. Always give back to your customers by putting some of your profit back into the business. This not only requires the basics of you, like continued education, and replacing outdated equipment. It also requires you thinking up new and improved ways to capture your audience through marketing, promotions, and guarantees. Watching your business grow with every effort that you put into it will be one of the most powerful and rewarding things you will ever accomplish.

And finally: are you ready for your business to grow very quickly? Whether you live in a small town or large city, the fastest and most cost-effective forms of marketing are also the ones that are the biggest kept secrets. The following information could catapult you from your current income level to a much higher one very quickly. The first is nothing more than assuming the role of a Public Relations Management for your own business. Write a few samples of interest stories that local publications would benefit from running in their paper or magazine. The story doesn't have to be a direct sell of your business, in fact it's not recommended. Instead you can offer public interest pieces about events you host, or write informative articles about the benefits of massage, trends in spa treatments, etc. and quote yourself as an expert in these articles. If your article is inspiring to the publications editorial staff, it will either be used immediately or put on file for a later date. You can send as many of these articles as you like. And here's the best part: the staff LOVES it when a good writer sends them pre-written articles. It makes their job a whole lot easier. Many don't change the article at all, but use it as is. Most just change a few words. I've heard this straight from the mouth of a very reputable journalist. In fact, she claims that if you become a reliable source of news angles, your plugs will rise to the top of the stack indefinitely. Some large magazines will PAY for a well-written article. (That's a nice side benefit of self-promotion!) Your articles could become a rotating feature in the publication. In small towns this type of marketing is very effective. There may be only one or two local publications. Human-interest stories are a main staple of these papers. Smaller communities need news worthy content. You may be the business in town that provides it for them, while simultaneously building your reputation. There will be little competition. Local radio shows too, in fact.

The second type of marketing that is equally effective in small or large communities, I like to refer to as "direct advertising". I came up with this name for it because it is the only form of advertising that every dollar that you put into it comes back to you as 100% profit. Never an advertising dollar is lost. Profit is guaranteed. How can this be, you ask? And why hasn't anyone told you this before? Because, then you would be at the top, and there's only so much room there. So people in the know don't tell you. What I am about to tell you is already very common practice. Massage Therapists with less skill may be making significantly more money than you by implementing this method.

Direct advertising requires you to provide a referral fee or an equivalent amount of massage to any professional who refers you clients. So, rather than typical advertising where placing an ad in a newspaper for $1000 a month may put you $400 in debt; you can provide a professional up to $750 (in money, gift certificates, or massage trade) for every $5,000 worth of business referred to you. Some examples of professionals already referring massage for their clients are: alternative health care providers, injury lawyers, hotel and condo concierge, limo drivers, yoga instructors and personal trainers, mid wives and travel agents, just to name a few. It is my understanding that some health care providers and/ or lawyers are prohibited from accepting this type of compensation in some U.S. states. Other states you'll find this to be common practice. Be sure to educate yourself on any laws in your state or country. Client referrals may be an acceptable form of repayment instead.

The less-expensive option for you is to refer clients to these trusted professionals. However, because your client base is often much smaller than theirs, you may not be able to refer as much volume as they will. To balance this relationship, and keep your referring professionals happy, they need to be compensated in some way. For many of these professionals, referring their clients to an MT who will provide them with superior quality treatment will be enough. Direct advertising covers your bases for those who don't find it adequate.

My hope in revealing the secret of direct advertising is to elevate the underpaid Massage Therapists, who have excellent hands-on ability, to an acceptable income level. I would love to see true healers succeed at this profession. Every day, Massage Therapists who do not have "the gift" rake in plenty of money through intelligent advertisement. Shouldn't you, with your amazing hands-on ability and desire to help people, be at least equally rewarded? The answer to that is: yes you should, and this is how you will; because without understanding how to advertise most effectively, word will never get out about you. And if the word never gets out about you and your phenomenal abilities, you won't make enough to stay in this profession very long. And that would mean one less healer following their chosen path in this world. We don't want that. Have you seen the state of the world? We need our healers, teachers, visionaries, rescuers, saviors, and saints to be healthy and well provided for. We need you. So get off your butt and do what scares you. Tell anyone and everyone you know that you need to be in contact with the aforementioned list of reputable people. Set up meetings with them. Sell your abilities and your passion. Then let them know that if they decided to refer to you, not only would you impress their referrals to no-end, you will also be saying thank you with a 15% referral fee (in gift certificates, cash, or other), if they so choose. They will love you. Not only are you a great healer, you are a savvy businessperson. What an admirable mixture of traits. The professionals in your life will find you a breath of fresh air.

I know you don't want people sending you massages because you compensate them. You want people to send you massages because you are a talented Massage Therapist. We all do. But this ship sailed a long time ago. It's time to jump aboard. In a perfect world perhaps it would be different. But really, what does it matter? Aren't you here to heal as many people as possible and to affect as many lives as positively as you can, in your short time on this planet? Is how you advertise to get to that goal really the focus here? I certainly don't think so. And I sincerely hope you can get past your biases and give my suggestions a try. PR management, the web, and direct advertising: tools of 21st century success.

"We begin life with the world presenting itself to us as it is. Someone - our parents, teachers, analysts - hypnotizes us to "see" the world and construe it in the "right" way. These others label the world, attach names and give voices to the beings and events in it, so that thereafter, we cannot read the world in any other language or hear it saying other things to us. The task is to break the hypnotic spell, so that we become undeaf, unblind and multilingual, thereby letting the world speak to us in new voices and write all its possible meanings in the new book of our existence. Be careful in your choice of hypnotists."

- Sidney Jourard

7

WORK OUTSIDE THE BOX

You have chosen a unique profession in that it has only recently gained mainstream popularity in the Western world. And not until very recently has it begun to define itself as a legitimate healing art and a medical necessity. Offhand, I can think of no other career choice that fully compares, in terms of uniqueness, to that of Massage Therapy. And yet many Massage Therapists approach this profession with the idea that it will be much like any other 9-to-5-job (Except that they may be free to do whatever they want). Do you see the obvious irony of this? Laziness and success do not mix. If you truly want to be successful you'll have to work for it. I will help you to work smarter and not harder, but there will still be some compromises along the way. We all have to make them. Probably only one in a billion Massage Therapists get handed the opportunity to work between the hours of 9:00 and 5:00 every day and earn $100 an hour fresh out of school. The rest of us have to earn that right. It may not take long, but it will take some choices that you may think you are dead set against. But I learned a long time ago to never say "Never".

Ah... the typical 9-to-5 Monday through Friday shift. This would be the ideal, right? Or would it? I encourage you to open your mind for a moment and weigh the argument that this is not likely to be the schedule of availability that will bring you the most success or allow you to work the least hours. Your average client works a lot, at least forty hours per week. I have clients who work eighty hours per week and when I massage them on a Saturday afternoon they assume I must not be doing so well financially, or that business has slowed down. It's funny to me. I work twenty hours a week or less, I take vacations whenever I want at the mere suggestion, and they somehow think that my schedule is unthinkable. I think the typical American grind is unthinkable, and I bet you do too.

Many Massage Therapists are attracted to this profession, in part, for the dream of creating their own schedules and not having to answer to anyone. Sadly, many of those same Massage Therapists aren't making enough money because they aren't working outside the box. They are holding on to an idea of how they wish this profession is structured, instead of embracing the reality of it. The truth is... today's client needs you when they can squeeze you into their hectic schedule. This is typically weekends and after work and often last minute. Is this what you want to hear? No, probably not. But it is the truth. Businesses like Nordstrom, 24-hour photo, fast food restaurants... in fact, most businesses and services in the U.S. emphasize speed and quality in their marketing. Luxury stores appealing to the masses have contributed to a nation of consumers who not only expect but demand VIP service, despite income level. They know what they want and they want it now. I don't see this trend ending any time soon. As our world's businesses become ever more efficient, you must follow this trend to prosper, especially while you are building clientele. Once you build your business to full capacity, you may decide to rein in your hours of operation. But at first, your goal is to think like one of those very service providers who make the profit from providing this type of high level of service. The most damaging attitude that you can take into this profession is that of the average North American consumer. You have to switch your mind-set. You are now the business owner with many, many competitors, not the consumer with ten dollars in your pocket and a grandiose sense of entitlement. Step into the role of a successful business owner, into the shoes of someone successful. They all have to make compromises, and willingly looked at those compromises as enjoyable choices to get where they are today. As Mary Engelbreit once so wisely said: "If you don't like something change it; if you can't change it, change the way you think about it."

There is no such thing as a typical week for me. Sure, I have rituals. I walk my Pomeranian every day, and practice myself-care regime. But my schedule is for me to decide. I may work every day for fourteen days straight, and not even realize it. I love what I do that much. And I do so little of it, it feels like fun, not work at all. Because I am willing to jump for those business travelers last minute, and see those tourists on Saturday morning, and devote a 6 PM timeslot to my VIP, I make enough money to be able to make choices about when I work and when I vacation. You can look at it as a sacrifice to work a couple of hours in the evenings and on weekends, or you can realize that it actually benefits you to do so.

You make more money when you do. You save more time when you make more money. Personally, I hate fighting the madness at the malls and post offices on weekends, and I despise going out on Saturday nights when venues are packed with drunken weekend warriors. So this schedule works well for me. I love that I can do all my errands midday, mid-week. I adore that I can do a massage in the morning, have lunch with a friend, do some shopping, yoga, sauna, see another last-minute client at six in the evening, and go on a date afterward. I especially love that I can do this every day for three weeks and then vacation somewhere warm and sunny. Working Monday through Friday is overrated, if you ask me. The problem, as I see it, is that everyone has been encouraged by society to think that a sixty-hour workweek with a hypothetical weekend off is better than a twenty-hour workweek with a few hours scattered through weekends and evenings. Riiggghhhttt! Do not fall into this line of thinking. Working fewer hours, and being well provided for is the goal. This is how you will be able to take care of your clients for many years to come.

You have a choice to be busy or not. Take any one of the routes that I will be presenting to you, and you will be a success. But if you want to work with celebrities, VIPS, and the highest paying clientele, you're going to have to be flexible with your schedule. No exceptions. Learn to look at it as freedom. Every time you say "Yes!" to a massage appointment, it provides you with that much more ability to say "no" when something truly worthwhile comes along. I know an LMT who has been complaining about being broke for years. Yet every time I've offered a massage there is typically a reason she says "No". The drive is too long, or she's hanging out with her friends, or she just doesn't feel like it. I don't understand it. I do understand that lazy feeling. I understand that self-defeating voice in your head. The one that says, "Oh, but I'm hanging out, I like this television program, I look terrible, it's cold outside, it's Saturday...." But if you listen to that voice, and act on it, you will not succeed at anything that takes self-motivation, this career included. You must say "YES! THANK YOU!" Get up off your bum, put a smile on your face, and be so grateful that you are about to pocket upwards of one hundred dollars an hour. A HUNDRED

DOLLARS AN HOUR! I mean, come on! If you can't be motivated by that, doing such a profoundly positive thing for people, then nothing will motivate you.

Think about it this way: If you were to say YES to just two extra massages a week, at the rate of $125 per massage (I'll explain in upcoming chapters how to earn this rate of pay), you would make an additional $12,000 per year. Now add an additional half an hour plus $15 tip to one of the massages for a total of $200. And two more $125 massages to your week. You have added an additional $27,600 to your yearly income. All you did was say "yes" four additional times per week for this extra money. And this is on top of an already light workweek. If you ask me, it's a no-brainer. That television program can wait. If you can adjust your thinking and societal programming on this point, you will make a lot of money, and have a lot of time on your hands. Don't let the nine-to-fivers talk you out of this one...you'll be making more money than them, and working half as much, in no time!

If you refuse to budge on this one point, I ask you to meet me halfway. Consider opening up a time slot for a client at 6 PM and cut an hour back from somewhere else, if you prefer. The 6 PM time slot will fill up immediately. Make sure that you fill it up with new clients or ones that can't see you at any other time due to work schedules. Don't schedule clients in this valuable time who have the ability to be flexible. You won't gain any additional business if you do, only lose an hour. It won't take long before you have a client in that time slot every day that you are available. Let's do the math: $100 per hour x 5 days per week x 4 weeks per month x11 months per year (we'll subtract 1 month for vacation time) = $22,000 per year additional income. Now, if I were you, I would go one step further and only schedule hour and a half appointments at that time slot. Up-sell to the client by telling them it is your most coveted time slot. Now you can add another $11,000 per year to your final income upping the total increase to $33,000 per year. Wow. Is that specific hour and a half every day so important that you would bring in $33,000 less every year because you refuse to work within it?

Remember the man that I told you about previously who dropped from $80,000-plus in the 80s to less than $24,000 in recent years? He refused to budge on his schedule. It was one more way in which he flat out denied the way in which this industry is evolving. He took it personally and thought it reflected a lack of appreciation for his healing abilities. Do not make the same mistake he did. For a few years I jumped and ran out the door to see clients. If they wanted an appointment NOW, either I would be the one to see them and develop a relationship with them, or they go elsewhere. It's as simple as that. Our clients often wait until the very last minute to schedule a massage. They will phone for an appointment two hours out, because they have a window of exactly two hours in between business meetings. Their neck is strained, they have a migraine and pseudo-sciatic pain is shooting down their right leg. Obviously, if you cannot see them, they will have no choice but to see someone else. It's not personal.

You have chosen a great profession to be able to step out of the rat race that our society currently defines as success. Now I am asking you to take that vision to the next level. Begin dismantling your society's views of which hours and times are acceptable to work and which are not. If you do, you will obtain a level of freedom that few people get to experience. The freedom of earning a great living, working few hours a week and having your work be rewarding and fun. Now that is my definition of the good life!

"I have always admired the ability to bite off more than one can chew and then chew it."

"William DeMille

8

REACH FOR THE "STARS"

If you are reading this, you must not be one of the Massage Therapists who have convinced themselves that the rich and famous don't need healing touch. Good for you! In the beginning of my career I often shot down suggestions of working with a more affluent clientele saying "They don't NEED my work. I want to work with the less fortunate." I now understand that this type of attitude is nothing more than wealth- discrimination. It is not in our job description to judge our client's lifestyle, fame, wealth, or lack of these luxuries. It is our job to facilitate healing within them. At the heart of each and every person lie the same troubles and fears. We are all human. EVERYONE needs healthy touch. Babies die without it, adults develop psychosis with out it. I believe that we are obligated, as healers, to offer treatment to all demographics of society, and to touch as many people's lives as we can in our short time on this planet.

However, having said that, I must admit working with the affluent has its advantages. The experiences, life lessons, and compensation that come with this side of the industry can be greatly rewarding. Better still, you'll find that once you are well compensated in this line of work, you have more time and resources to take care of the world in other ways. It's a whole lot easier to give free massages to charity, or abuse shelters, for example, when you are happy and healthy and well provided for by a clientele who can afford to pay you a fair rate for expert treatment.

You don't have to live in L.A. or New York to massage the stars. There are a couple of ways to build a celebrity clientele, in your city or town. The first is a route that a fellow Massage Therapist has mastered and turned into quite the niche for himself. He provides seated massage to his cities local film crews. Even if there isn't money in the film budget for his services, he can usually talk the Unit Production Manager into letting him bring a massage chair and offer massage for cash to the individuals on-site. The crew often works long, hard hours and are grateful for the service. This often leads to other opportunities and connections with the actors, directors, and producers as well, and provides an opportunity for you to pass out cards and schedule massages with them too. (Be set up for mobile massage for this group. They will most likely need you to travel on-site to the rental home or hotel that they are currently lodging.)

To build your own on-set seated massage business for the stars, I recommend going to www.writerdirector.com and scrolling down to your State Film Commission. There you will research any films that are currently being shot in your town or city. This is where you will find the contact info for the Unit Production Manager. Contact him with a brief proposal and list of previous experience that shows you to be reputable. Have a professional head shot included. Make sure that you edit out any errors! Your proposal is your only impression, so it must not be full of easy-to-remedy mistakes. Keep trying until you hear a "yes". Once that first film credit is on your resume, it will be a breeze to get future work with that film company again and easily open doors to others.

The second way to build a solid celebrity-VIP client base is to contract with reputable four-star hotels in your city. Are you ready for a roller coaster ride of experiences? Because that is precisely what you are going to get contracting Licensed Massage Therapy services to these hotels: the good, the bad and the ugly, as they say. In my opinion, there is no better way to acquire a celebrity clientele in any city (short of being born into a Hollywood family) than contracting with a four-star hotel. There is no better way to force yourself to stay on your toes, think fast, and all-around tighten your image than being a "beck and massage girl" for the Hollywood elite. Would I have changed a thing about my career as the celebrities' Massage Therapist? No. I have few regrets; life is too short. Was it always the easiest career path to follow? No, it wasn't. But it suited my personality better than any other path that I tried. I connected with my clients in a deeply profound way, I learned more about being a professional than in any other area of this profession, and I collected enough stories to fill more than one book.

Working in a four-star (or super-hip three-star) hotel will crack you up, blow you away, and thrill you to no end. These hotels are meant to evoke feelings that you are surrounded by people of power and affluence the minute you walk in the door. And let's face it, they are. They are the places where dreams come true. Are you into fashion? Then of course you will massage your favorite designer. Follow basketball? The NBA guys love you! Live for a good laugh? Massage the world's biggest comedian four days in a row and dine with him and the world's hottest band members at a local Italian restaurant. Sure! Why not? You may get invited around the world with your clients. I took a leap of faith and traveled to New York with a fashion model one week after massaging her for the first time. She is a great friend now. I been flown out-of-state for a $1,500 day rate and tipped $600 on top of it! I've been invited into celebrities' lives, dinners and backstage shows. I've had a super wealthy woman convince her husband to build me a spa, and invite me to live on their mansion's third floor, literally next door to the house of the President of the United States. I have kidded and joked with some of the most famous and sexiest actors in the world. I have turned down massages with some of the craziest celebrities in the world. I have also fallen on my ass in a mud puddle running to that next demanding client, had to take taxis through a snow blizzard to a single massage, been slandered by the most jealous and catty

Massage Therapists, and had to massage the egos of concierge with more skill than it ever took to please the most narcissistic of the Hollywood elite. This job has its ups and downs.

If you decide to enter this side of the industry, you'll have your work cut out for you from the get-go. Just getting your foot in the door of a reputable hotel can be tough. Either they have a fully-functioning spa and no room for outside contractors, or they have added an outside massage company to provide all Massage Therapists for the hotel, or they already have a list of Massage Therapists to choose from and many of them are ready to fight you to the ground so that you do not get their position in line. This last point was shocking to me when I first entered this industry. Why would healers be competitive with each other? I questioned. I realize now that it was easy for me to not understand such a mentality, because I had had a few lucky breaks that allowed me to showcase my abilities, which created a large number of repeat clients, which in turn built me a great reputation. That is not to say that I didn't work like a dog to get where I am, but I have seen others willing to work, not get the initial lucky breaks, and fail. Worse yet, I have seen many get the lucky breaks and not be willing to put everything into it required to succeed. What a waste. Those Massage Therapists, if educated about what was required of them, most likely would have stepped aside from the opportunities and created an opening for another Massage Therapist who was more than willing to go the extra mile for the same position. I plan on telling you everything there is to know about contracting through hotels, and also dispel a few myths. From there you can decide if it suits your personality or not. Myself, I can honestly say that the excitement, the challenges, the opportunities for growth, the influx of new people and the adventures were right up my alley. I am thrilled and honored to have lived this chapter of my life. I believe it has helped me grow into the woman I am today, and readied me for a much richer and more powerful life.

So how do you become a contractor for these hotels? First, do the basics: create a professional business card, make sure your name and number are the largest information on the card, create packets that include your card, massage license, and proof of liability insurance. Get your personal image down tight, and practice talking to intimidating people for a few days before you take the leap. For whatever reason, the concierge can be intimidating. You'll learn after a while that they are not, truly. They are insecure just like the rest of us. But at first, a few of them will make you squirm and second-guess yourself. Fake it till you make it. In fact, it never hurts to know of local great restaurants, current shows or events, or parties to spark their interest. So now you are armed and ready. First, ask everyone you know to connect you with anyone they know who works at a local reputable hotel. Seek connections through those individuals. Anyone in the food industry is a good bet. Servers and bartenders get to know their peers at hotels. Front desk manager connections are fantastic. Any concierge who is willing to introduce you to your city's concierge group, you should forever place on a pedestal. It doesn't matter that their particular hotel may not need you. It only matters that you are introduced to concierge who are employed by hotels that do. If you are really lucky, you'll get invited to the concierge parties and hobnob with them and get yourself at the top of the call list at your favorite hotel. You might think this sounds difficult, but it won't always be. I know of one LMT who is an absolute phony. She is terrible to anyone she feels threatens her business. I've seen her scream at spa employees, then turn around and behave calm and Zen-like with the hotel concierge ten minutes later... and she gets invited to these parties quite often. Apparently, she just didn't give up until she got her way. I was never invited to any of these events until my reputation was already established, but you're already in the know, so I suggest you work your magic from the very beginning.

If you have none of these connections, worry not; neither did I. Do your homework on the hotels, decide which have the highest caliber of guests (never contract for a lesser-rated hotel), call the concierge desk, introduce yourself, ask who the head concierge is, and schedule a time to drop off your information. Bring extra copies for the other concierge who is not present. Take down their names and find time to meet with them as well. Upon meeting them, smile a genuinely warm smile. Present yourself with confidence. Chat the concierge up about a fabulous new restaurant or current event. Give them the sense that you will please their clients (if you do, it means positive feedback and higher tips from clients for them). Let them know that you are able to be there in an hour, or two, reasonably. Tell them that you provide the current going rate for referral fees. Wittily let them know that you can rest when you're dead. That massage is your life. Assure them that their clients will love you. Also add that you don't see late-night clients without prior approval from them, and that if you are ever hit on or made to feel uncomfortable in any way, you will end the massage and bill for the full treatment time. And you expect the hotel to back you on this policy. After that last comment their demeanor will change to very serious and upright and respectful, and you've got them right where you want them. Now make your exit. Let them know your schedule is packed, you don't want to take up any more of their time, and you appreciate their meeting with you. "I'll look forward to your call," you will say as you are walking out the door, waving goodbye.

You are all they can think about: for five minutes, a day or a maybe even a week (you're so in, your outfit must have been fabulous, and your banter dead on). Then their reality sinks in, and they get busy and massages are rolling in, and they keep calling the same Massage Therapists on the list. It's not personal. It's habit.

They are comfortable with these tried and true MTs. Also, depending on the hotel, they may not have a massage to give you for a whole week. You need to figure out which hotel can provide you with two a day or more. Get to the top of that hotel's list. Once you are called in, arrive early to get an accurate idea of how each individual hotel does things. Do the guests sign the massage charge onto the room and you get paid immediately afterward, or every thirty days? Is there a massage room and equipment provided by the hotel, or do you provide all necessities? Is parking compensated? Are you required to have an invoice with their logo printed on it, or will a general one do? Try to keep an updated and accurate file of this information and commit it to memory. Bring in your massage licensing and insurance renewals every year, before they have to ask for it. It's the little stuff that elevates you to the top of the call list.

Ahhh, the top of the call list: where all the massages are offered to you first and appointments scheduled a month in advance are dropped in your lap. It is the envy of all ten MTs below. How do you get there? From what I've observed there are three ways. 1) You can earn this position by always being available at the drop of a hat (carry your cell phone with you everywhere, no exceptions), receiving rave reviews from your clients, maintaining professional but fun relationships with your referring concierge, and being cooperative and friendly with your fellow Massage Therapists (even when they are not to you). 2) You can befriend or encourage a concierge to be attracted to you. I wouldn't recommend this route. I see other Massage Therapists do it successfully more than I care to admit, but personally know it would blow up in my face. Besides, call me old-fashioned, but I like the sense of self-satisfaction that comes with an earned reputation. 3) You can bribe the concierge. As I mentioned earlier, there is a going rate that you give as a gratuity to each and every concierge that sends you business. It's generally 20% maximum of the massage rate, tip not considered. Every LMT who contracts from hotels is expected to pay this "gratuity". If they do not, they will not work. I have seen Massage Therapists get angry over this and cry over the injustice, but the reality is... it is your direct advertising budget. You are getting a 100% return on your money, and you simply can't get that any other way. You want to talk about injustice... place an ad in your local telephone book stacked against all your competitors and realize at the end of the year you lost thousands of dollars. That is injustice. If you have issues with semi-enforced referral fees for concierge who refers business to you, don't bother contracting with hotels. Having said this, however, the standard rate agreed upon should be honored by all contracting Massage Therapists. There is an obvious reason for this. Once the bribing begins, it will never end. After awhile the concierge will be pocketing more profit for a booked massage than the MTs' profit and this side of the industry will be ruined for everyone.

For twenty years, Seattle's LMTs knew and understood to not tip more than the other contracting LMTs. The ones who wanted more business chose one of the first two routes to get it. Then recently a new Licensed Massage Therapist thought it was a brilliant idea to incrementally increase the amount of money she was giving the concierge, to undercut the rest of us. Fortunately, my own clientele was well established by then, and I was doing okay. But I watched what it did to the other Massage Therapists. Nothing was offered them but leftovers. Their bank accounts began to dwindle, even in an upward economy. I knew that this decision she had made would forever disrupt the integrity of the industry, and that it was only a matter of time before other Massage Therapists would feel forced to have to break the twenty-year pact of honor. One by one they fell. Massage Therapists gave a little more here, a little more there, profit margins went down, and hotels brought in massage companies to take over when upper management discovered the rampant bribery being expected from a select group of concierge. Profits sank even lower. Eventually, the Massage Therapist who began the bribing fell dramatically on the call list. She wasn't available enough with her newly growing family, and wasn't tipping any more than anyone else. So she upped the ante. She created more clever "games" and "contests", thinly veiled means to "squash the competition". And the games began.

The economy later declined and Massage Therapists in the hotel industry did one of three things: 1) went broke, 2) switched careers, or 3) bribed their dignity away. The exceptions were those Massage Therapists who had followed my golden rule, which I suggest you memorize from the beginning: "Never depend on business from the hotels. Hotel massage is a luxury service. It is the icing on the cake. The cake is composed of health insurance clients, PIP and L&I claim work, and a devoted clientele. These are the things that last through a weak economy. People need healthcare regardless of economic stability." Those Massage Therapists forming the exception were few and far between. Most chose instead to fight and claw their way to the top over and over, while the concierge's wallets got fatter. I suggest you do not be the one to start this descent by bribing your way to the top. It will only backfire in the end. Earn a solid reputation based on outstanding performance and additional services offered to increase value. It will eventually lead you towards much greater opportunities.

A key part of working with hotels is establishing relationships with concierge. As I've stated, there are different ways to do this, and of course each relationship that you build with individual concierges will be unique. I hope that in telling you of the compensation systems that have been put in place, you are not of the impression that every concierge is greedy. While it's true that there are a few bad eggs that stink up the entire henhouse, there are typically more concierges than not focused on the well being and satisfaction of the hotel guest first, and the fatness of their wallet second. Generally speaking, if there is a head concierge staffed with a particular hotel, it's less likely that rampant overt bribery will slip through the cracks, although not always. I've noticed that friendships formed with these individuals will catapult the worst Massage Therapists to the top. Remember the phony I was telling you about? She's a friend of the head concierge at a busy hotel.

The difference between the two extremes of concierges' integrity is outstanding. On one side you have the concierge who calls you because of your reputation, he honors and respects your individualism and drive to succeed, and he often refuses to accept the going rate of commission saying, "are you sure this isn't too much?" On some level, he's right. How much is a single phone call worth, really? On the other side, you have the concierge who repeatedly hits on you, your success threatens him, you're expected to bribe him, he dictates what amount of gratuity is expected, he monitors how much income you bring in from the hotel he works for, and decreases your appointment volume when it appears your income may exceed his. The single phone call he sends you is worth your dignity, basically. If you contract with hotels, you can expect to work with these two types of concierges and everything in between. The light at the end of the tunnel is this: eventually the jerks get fired. Or so I'd like to believe. Mine did. Remember to always hold your head up high. Make their job as easy as possible. Foresee any problems and fix them before they happen. Be early, or at least on time. Smile, but don't be insincere. Be nice, but don't be a doormat. Look sharp. Think fast. If you do, you'll develop some pretty cool bonds with these professionals. If any of them pull ego trips on you, remember this: few people dream of becoming a concierge when they are kids. Most likely they are not totally happy with their jobs, and it threatens them that they perceive you to have obtained a level of freedom that they don't have. We are all on a journey together. Try to be understanding, though at times it may not be easy do so.

Speaking of feeling threatened: let's talk about Massage Therapists who only work with hotels. Originally they had other means of predictable income. Perhaps they supplemented with hotel work on the side. But after turning down massages for $125 an hour only to be paid $150 for a whole day's work, they began to rethink things. They dropped their other massage gigs and got into full-time hotel work. The lack of vision behind this is detrimental because 1) This type of massage is the first thing to go in recession, 2) it is entirely dependent on whether or not the concierge call you, 3) the work is seasonal, summers may be crammed while winters lull, 4) because your clientele is primarily from out of town, they won't contribute to your reputation or increase your clientele where you live, 5) it requires always being on your toes, dropping everything last minute, and scheduling a life for yourself can be nearly impossible. All the hotel MTs marvel at this. You could sit by the phone all day with no calls for massage. The minute you go to the gym, the sun comes out, you meet a friend for drinks or your kid gets sick... that's when the phone rings and a client needs you immediately. It's the nature of "easy" money. You pay in other ways, I suppose.

So there is this group of Massage Therapists are hanging out in a metaphorical kiddy pool together, all wanting to stretch their legs. It's comical when you are able to stand outside of it to see each one manipulating, lying, tricking or abusing to get more room in that tiny pool. There are, of course, always a few standing outside the pool, satisfied with dipping a toe in and remaining unscathed. But when you're in that pool with them, it is anything but amusing. It hurts, if you let it. I suggest you consider yourself warned, and don't take it personally. In the past I had always worked with Massage Therapists who believed in there being "enough for everyone", similar to my belief, so at first this behavior was shocking. In fact, most of the Massage Therapists in the hotel industry verbally express the same belief, but many of their actions screamed loud and clear their true belief: "I don't have enough, and it is your fault!" The fiercely competitive nature of this side of the industry changes people, and it will try to change you. Don't let it happen to you. Again, protect yourself by bringing in enough money to cover your bills with Insurance work, PIP and L&I claims and personal clients. Let the hotel work be the icing on your cake. No exceptions. If you do, it could be one of the most rewarding experiences you will ever have.

Another thing that you shouldn't take personally: clients who hit on you, because it's not personal. I'm going to try to explain to you why men ask for a massage, and expect something sexual. I am in no way condoning this behavior from these men. But I do feel it's necessary for you as a professional to have a well-rounded understanding of the thought process involved in these scenarios, so that you can truly understand how NOT personal it is. You can learn how to handle these situations with grace and dignity. My understanding is that our profession is misunderstood as being sexual for a variety of reasons: 1) Lack of education in the general populace. This is becoming less common, and typically doesn't apply to high-end hotels where the guests tend to be highly educated. 2) Due to prostitution being illegal in the US, versus tolerated by other countries, many prostitutes here are forced to advertise by using cover-ups. Unfortunately for us, Massage Therapy seems to be the most common. 3) There still are massage "parlors" around, and as long as there are, we will receive unwanted advances. 4) National massage standards make getting a license in certain states a walk in the park, establishing poorly trained Massage

Therapists with no ability to provide medical treatment, and a quick way for a prostitute to get a genuine massage license as a cover – a perfect example for why massage accreditation standards should be nationalized. 5) There are licensed MTs, possibly working next door to you, who offer sexual favors for additional money. Even reputable fashion magazines write articles about how "happy endings" are common practice in cities such as LA. I know, it sounds pretty disheartening, right? But remember how I told you that I rarely get hit on any more? It's the truth. I want to be as honest as possible with you so you can be armed with education. I feel that this subject is commonly "swept under the rug" and new Massage Therapists are left vulnerable to inappropriate advances in the workplace.

There are a couple of indicators that someone is looking for more than a massage even before they book the appointment. Know them to be prepared: 1) a client asks, while booking the appointment, what the MT looks like and/or how old he/she is. 2) The client books an hour and a half or longer "light pressure" massage with an MT he's previously never seen before. 3) The client asks about draping practices or makes reference to massage in "Thailand", which is typically a reference to visiting massage "parlors". 5) A client keeps asking for appointments with new Massage Therapists, after being sent the very best (thus perhaps he's looking for something no one is willing to give him). Further signs, once you've entered the treatment room, are: The unsubtle head to toe body look over. A wad of $100 bills within view and/or a romantic scene set in the room. And tip-offs once they are on the table: they refuse to close their eyes, but instead look at you. They move their body in inappropriate ways (e.g. gyrating hips, or commonly men will spread their legs until they are about to fall off the table while they are lying face down.) They might try to persuade you to discuss anything that will break down your boundaries, such as your marital status, anything sexual, or accuse you of being "too professional" and in need of "letting loose a little". While these examples may feel a little graphic for you, again, I feel you need to know the signs. When this is happening to you, the worst part about it is that you are being manipulated. Most of it is so subtle that it feels as if you may be misconstruing their meaning, and you might be...so it's necessary to not over-react. If you learn to enter the room with confidence and a no-nonsense attitude, you will avoid these scenarios as much as possible. The last time I had anything like this happen to me was over two years ago. Strangely, it wasn't unpleasant because the man was very straightforward, not manipulative at all, and as a result allowed me to remain in control of the situation. The interaction went something like this: (Client) "I would like to be very straightforward with you and ask you a question. In no way do I intend to offend you with this question, and I will honor and respect your answer whatever it may be. If you say "no" I will not bring it up again." After I told him to proceed he asked, "Do you give full-release massage?" I answered "No. But I respect you asking me outright rather than being passive-aggressive about what you want. I understand how commonplace this has become in L.A. (where he lived), so I don't take your request personally. However, if you make me uncomfortable in any way, from this moment forward, I will leave the room, security will get my belongings, and you will be billed for the full amount." Strange as it sounds, the rest of the massage went quite well. I appreciated his honest forthright communication, as did he. He never made me feel the slightest bit uncomfortable after that conversation. Personally, I didn't consider this interaction a violation nearly as much as when clients had tried to manipulate me in the past. But if something like this happens to you, only you will be able to judge how you feel about it, and what the appropriate reaction is. You'll know by the feeling in your gut. Follow that instinct. Get in tune with it. It may steer you clear of the "bad guys" even before you schedule the appointment. I now know the minute I hear the person say, "I'd like to schedule a massage" if they are looking for "extras". If they are a particularly big creep, I now know just seeing their name on a schedule. It triggers a response in me. A loud, angry siren goes off in my head screaming "pervert!" and I absolutely refuse to see that person. I have risked losing my contracting positions because of it. But I KNOW. And I will not compromise. So, that's that. I suggest you don't schedule with people you feel funny about. Be firm with those that are slightly pushing your personal boundaries, they may just need to know what those boundaries are before being able to respect them. Walk out on those who overtly hit on you and treat you with disrespect. You are not a healer to be sexually victimized. You do not touch people to have them prey on you. You know this so don't be afraid to act on it. Enter each session with the thought that you have clear and clean energy and, in turn, so should they. If you follow these guidelines, you'll be surprised how little this will happen to you at all.

I chose to write about this "type" of client in the chapter on hotel massage, not because you will get hit on in hotels more than anywhere else, but because people assume you will. When I was unsure of myself and had personal healing to do in the early days of my career, I was hit on everywhere: by my employers, my clients, at job interviews, on the street. Not a nice "can I take you to dinner" kind of hit on, but in an intimidating, sleazy kind of way. Later, I discovered that one can not necessarily predict which hotel or chiropractor's office or salon will bring more of this your way. Unfortunately, it's a trial and error kind of discovery process. And don't be too quick to judge... the highest-rated, uber-conservative, "old money" hotel brought the most undesired situations my way, while the lesser-rated competitor hotel with an overtly sexy image brought none. ZERO incidences in FIVE years. As with anything, you can't judge a book by its cover. Look how different this one turned out from your original expectations!

So now that we've put to rest your greatest fears about working in hotels, let's get to the basics of how to ensure this rewarding experience is an easy and profitable venture for you. Most importantly: be prepared. As was mentioned earlier, carry your cell phone with you everywhere. A missed call is not only missed money, it's missed future calls from that concierge, and you can't afford it. They generally cannot wait for you to call back, as the guests want immediate confirmation. So get used to excusing yourself in the middle of anything to answer that call! Have a massage table, extra sets of clean sheets, massage lotion bottles, and a gallon of massage lotion with a pump top for refills in your trunk. If you offer specialty massage such as hot stone, carry that equipment with you as well. I learned to size down to a tiny crock pot that fit four stones at a time, in order to provide a version of the service for out-call clients. Keep a receipt book, business cards, and massage lotion, and iPod or CDs in a professional carry bag. Your massage table should be covered, and on wheeled cart at all times. Never enter the massage room hauling a big table over your shoulder. It's unsightly, unprofessional, and makes the client sympathize with you, which is not a good thing. Make sure the bag is slightly larger than the width of your table, so that you can fit a once folded over thin sheepskin cover for additional table comfort. Don't bother bringing a bolster when you can just as easily use a pillow off a hotel bed, no need for a blanket when the hotel provides one, or a thick robe will do just as well. Pare down to the basics, buy only the highest quality, lightest versions, and leave anything else in the trunk of your car. There is no reason to carry in a bulky pile of stuff into the hotels. If you do, you look like a bag lady, and it is entirely overwhelming to the client's senses. If you can afford to, I highly recommend purchasing an Ultra-Lite table with aluminum legs. The weight difference is astoundingly easier to manage. After purchasing mine, my mood elevated because I was no longer in pain after hoisting a heavy table in and out of my trunk all day. I picked mine up on eBay for only $299 new. Scour Craigslist www.craigslist.com, eBay www.ebay.com, and massage school sales boards for new or slightly used tables, and save yourself 50% or more. Or, if your budget allows, purchase a new one at: www.amazon.com. Find direct links to these sites at my own www. hundredthousanddollarmassage.com. The best part is that the energy that you save from not having to carry around an additional twenty pounds of stuff to each massage, you'll be able to do one more massage each day with ease. Why carry all this in your trunk, you ask? Why not just grab some sheets and a table from home? It doesn't work that way.

How it more likely works is...you pick up a call from a hotel concierge, while a client is getting on the table at your office. They set you up for an appointment thirty minutes after your current appointment ends, which is perfect timing to get to the hotel and set up. You call your friend to cancel lunch plans. After your office session ends, ready to jump in the car and head to your hotel appointment, you notice you have a missed call. It's the hotel concierge apologizing that the guest has declined the massage. They called while you were on the phone with your friend, but your phone didn't beep. You call your friend back; luckily she can still make lunch. While you're in the middle of your lunch in the sun, at your favorite restaurant with your best friend, the concierge calls back... you guessed it... the guest changed their mind "how soon can you be here?" the concierge asks. You ask for the check and jump in the car to weave through lunch-hour traffic to get to this client. You jump out of the car with four minutes to get inside the hotel and you open the trunk. There's nothing in the trunk. You just lost this particular hotel account. Ouch. You get my point. Be prepared. You will rarely know what, when, or where, so be on your toes. I suggest four or more sets of clean sheets in the trunk just in case, even if you aren't at the top of a call list. The day that someone call in sick and they have four massages back to back for you will most likely be the day that you forgot to restock your laundry. Oh the irony! It's the stuff of Alanis Morissette songs.

I know, better than anyone, that contracting massage services to hotels can be overwhelming. But that's only a small part of the time. If you have made it to the end of this chapter and still want to give it a try, I highly recommend it. If you are someone who thrives on adventure, loves to meet new people, and gets easily bored... this is the niche market for you. Imagine: Running from here to there in the thick of the urban jungle, mannequins tempting you with colorful treasures in every window you fly past. Your fabulous designer flats clink along the sidewalk. The doorman smiles and knows you by name at the hottest hotel in the city. Your favorite celebrity client awaits you in his room, and upon opening the door he greets you with a warm hug and says, "It's so good to see a friend". About this time you will think to yourself, "Thanks for the heads up, Meagan". And I am saying to you now, "You are so very welcome, my dear."

"Put your future in good hands. Your own."

- Author unknown

9

BIG $$$ MASSAGE

By now you've figured out that I believe there are very few paths to success in this profession while working for someone else. The nature of this work is financially limiting when working for an employer because your small profit margin is divided. And while there is typically a high cost per hour for massage services, there are very few hours that can and should be worked in a day. And of course, the ideal is for you to work less and make more, not the other way around. While at first you may be conservative in building your business and branching out, eventually your goal is to leave any situation that requires you to give more than twenty massages per week to have a satisfactory income level. This will allow you to give massage for many years, thus increasing your profit margin greatly. It's timely and expensive to have to re-educate yourself because your wrists, elbows, or morale have been broken from giving too much. It has happened to some of the best Massage Therapists; don't let it happen to you.

Always consider your profit margin before accepting a contracting position. Consider any additional expenses that decrease your amount of pay. Parking costs, rental fees, vehicle needs, gas prices, transportation costs, equipment requirements, uniform cleaning bills, and advertising can decrease your once high profit margin to dust if you aren't careful. Employers lure Massage Therapists into their web with $30 an hour compensation and medical benefits. But those same employers may only be able to provide you with less than four hours work per day while requiring you to clean office areas or do laundry for a minimum wage rate in between appointments. Your cost of lunch in between, gas and car mileage to get to and from the work site, and fitting their dress requirements can often leave you trying to live off $2,500, after taxes, per month. At that rate, you'll be lucky to pay off your school loans in fifty years, you'll be living a life you don't love, and you'll burn out fast. This is not what I want for you. I want you to work twenty hours a week, and bring in an excess of money so that you will easily be able to provide medical insurance for your family out of your own pocket, if necessary. Side note: Your medical insurance is a tax write-off at the end of the year, so you will essentially make that money. As will be explained in my blog. You can access it at yep, you guessed it: www.hundredthousanddollarmassage.com.

I want for you to be well provided for. I want you to give massages that bring top dollar every time, so that your health and mind are happy and fulfilled. $100K per year is an average of twenty massages per week at an average of $100 per hour. It's easier to reach this $100 average than you can imagine. Begin by taking extended education courses to increase your marketability. This is a fantastic way to be able to offer your clients greater value and be able to reasonably raise your rates above the average. Additional training in Cranial Sacral work, Trager, Rolfing, Feldenkrais, or Reiki for example can corner you in a market as an expert of these modalities and increase your cost of service by 25% or more. Here in Seattle, a typical massage would run about $65 per hour, while an expert in any of these treatments can easily charge $85 per hour. While specialty massage modalities (approx $85 per hour) and outcall-massage (approx. $115 per hour) can bring in the average of $100 per hour that is required to earn $100K in twenty hours per week, it will take time to develop a devoted clientele. There are two forms of injury massage that provide a high rate of repeat appointments, even before you have built yourself a regular clientele. They are PIP (Personal Injury Protection), and L&I (Labor and Industries) injury treatment massage. These pay approximately $88 to $131 per hour for injury treatment massage performed. (This is information based on my local region. Yours may be different. A small amount of researching your region's specifics under the UCR or customary rates via Google will lead you to current information.) Becoming a provider for either of these mediums is much easier than you may suspect. I will walk you through the steps to be able to bill these companies, because I find that many Massage Therapists are unsure of how to begin billing for either of these mediums. But first, a quick explanation of each of them is in order.

A PIP claims is filed by a person who has been injured in an auto accident. Their medical bills are covered by their (or the other driver's) auto insurance coverage. To be able to treat these individuals they must first get a prescription for massage from their doctor or chiropractor. Typically the doctor will write it for twelve treatments or less and write more if the patient is reevaluated and found to need more treatment.

An L&I claim is filed by an employee who has been injured in his / her workplace. For example, I have massaged recipients of L&I benefits who had a metal plate fall on their head, one who fell off a ladder, and a nurse who was given whiplash by a 230-pound child suffering from autism. Plan on working with a wide variety of injuries with L&I claims. In each case the injured client has filed a claim with his work, seen a doctor, and that doctor has written a prescription (script) for a certain number of Massage Therapy treatments. Typically the doctor has written in the client's areas of pain and injury that need to be treated by the MT. After the initial prescription is fulfilled, you are not covered to provide massage treatment for your patient until she or he is reevaluated and prescribed more massage treatments by their physician.

To bill for PIP claim clients in Washington is a relatively simple process. Do any and all necessary research so that you are aware of any differences in your state or country. Have your client fill out all necessary initial evaluation forms. Make sure they provide all their current personal information, any pertinent claim information such as insurance company name, policy number, and claim representative name and extension. Call the claims representative and establish a relationship with him or her immediately. Find out whether the client has been found at fault for the accident or not. If they have, you need to watch closely that you don't exceed the client's coverage amount. It can be used up quickly when other health care providers are working with the client simultaneously. If the client exceeds his benefits, he is obligated to pay his remaining bills out of pocket, and usually can't, leaving you stuck with the bill... so watch it. More typically I find that drivers who are the innocent party seek treatment. They are usually the ones who were hit, and often suffer more severe symptoms.

While you are treating your client, document all findings on SOAP charts. Keep track of any progress made with the client's range of motion as well as reductions in pain, inflammation, adhesions, spasms, etc. When you have fulfilled the number of massages on the prescription, fill out a Health Insurance Claim Form (otherwise known as a HICFA) and mail all pertinent paperwork to the claim rep handling payment. It typically helps to add a cover letter with your logo kindly requesting payment within thirty days. By law, auto insurance companies have thirty days to pay you, however I find you have to be proactive to make this happen 100% of the time. I call the claim rep fourteen days after mailing the billing to him/her to check up on the status of the billing. My conversation typically goes something like this: "Hi, This is Meagan Holub. I'm Mary Smith's Massage Therapist. Her claim number is 5551212. I've been treating her for the August 11th auto accident. I know how tremendously busy you must be, but I sent a billing statement to you about two weeks ago and I wanted to make sure that I provided all the information you need to process the bill within the next couple of weeks." They will sometimes reply defensively, sometimes gratefully: "Oh, I haven't been able to look at that yet, but I'll move it to the top of my pile," or, "What is their claim number? I'll look it up now," or, "Oh, that case has been moved to a new claims representative. Here's his number." You may have to make a few more calls, leave a few messages, but you will be paid within thirty days. I guarantee it. Even better, they seem to add a note to your file that says to do so next time. After a while, the checks roll in like clockwork without you calling.

It is common for auto insurance companies to be billed up to $120 per hour, or $30 per "unit" which is comprised of fifteen minutes each for Massage Therapy. "Unit" is found on line 24G of your HICFA form. Never exceed 60 minutes, or four units of treatment in a day, and never provide massage outside of injury treatment modalities. And never bill more than your current cash rate. (So, if you provide outcall massage at a rate of $120 per hour, you may also bill the insurance at that rate. If you bill $85 per our in-studio, likewise you would bill $85 per hour). You may not get reimbursed if you don't follow these guidelines. Also, if you add fifteen minutes or one "unit" of Hydrotherapy (a hot wet pack on the injured area) to your treatment session you can bill for it at $19 per unit. This can bring you in a maximum amount of $139 per treatment for PIP claims when figuring in regular massage treatment rates. At first you will see these clients 2-3 times per week, per the doctor's prescription, and later on the treatments will slow down to once a week before treatment completion. In the ten years that I have been seeking to be reimbursed through PIP claims, I have only not been paid once, and that was for a client I should never have agreed to work with in the beginning. He was a friend of a friend's family member, and was known to be a smooth talker and a bit of a crook, and well... lesson learned.

Remember to find out your client's maximum injury protection coverage amount and stay informed of the balance with their representative. If you do, this is a great way to make excellent money and help people heal some pretty significant injuries. On a side note: the client's claim rep may ask you personal questions about your client to try to get you to spill the beans on them. Even something as simple as, "How is Mary feeling?" Although it sounds like concern, NEVER directly answer this question. If you were to say, "Oh much better, thank you," the rep will document that in her file, and later your client my have their treatment cut short, or have your words used against him/her when settling in court. I have a friend who is a claims rep. She helped me to understand that it is claim reps' first priority to limit the amount of money that is provided to the client, if at all possible. Remember that when dealing with any of them. Many insurance companies are profit-motivated first and foremost. Despite their advertisements claiming people come first, according to my friend, quite often it's their bottom line that does.

I think the best thing about working with auto accident victims is the close bond you build with these clients, as they are in tremendous pain and experiencing a plethora of symptoms when they have their first appointment with you. By the last appointment, more often than not, many changes have occurred in their health and their life, all of which were shared with you along the way. The one perceived downfall of treating PIP clients is that your billings don't come back right away. In fact, you may work with one client for months before being reimbursed at all. The bright side of this, however, is that when you are paid, the checks are rather large. I use these as savings accounts for my slow season from October through January. I put any PIP checks in my savings account and use it during these months so that I am able to spend generously all year long. I love large checks being delivered to my mailbox. I think you will too.

Billing for Labor & Industries clients in Washington is a bit more of a process. But not a difficult one if you are guided through it, which I am about to do for you. Here in Washington State, you'll need to apply with Labor and Industries to be a provider for them. To do so, you will need a NPI (National Provider Identification), to obtain one you will go to the National Plan Provider Enumeration System Homepage at: http://nppes.cms.hhs.gov/, then click on the "How to apply" link and it will walk you through how to apply via internet, email or phone. After you apply, you may have to wait a few weeks for the number so make sure you time this in advance of applying with Labor and Industries. Again, check your state or county's specific requirements before proceeding. You can easily access information through your local state or province government web page.

Once you have your NPI you are ready to apply to become an L&I provider. Labor and Industries last paid me $113 per 60 minute massage. Rumor has it that L&I will be lowering their compensation to $88 per hour here very soon. Which is fair if you are only providing treatment from your studio and comparatively pricing with your other specialty massage rates (It may no longer be feasible to provide the mobile services your clients at the $88 rate, but it still goes a long way towards your $100 per hour average.) Always stay on top of ay changes, legal, or otherwise, initiated by any insurance provider that you bill. L&I only accepts the HICFA form for billing. When you send your complete HICFA form, also enclose copies of the client's prescription and L&I claim form. The process is very streamlined. However, on the down side, they have up to 90 days to pay you. (Sometimes it seems they count down the days before mailing your check.) To become an L& I provider, I suggest you skip the middle steps and call directly. Request the provider application and instructions be mailed to you. Labor and Industries Washington can be found at: www.lni.gov./ under the "Contact Information" link. For you Washingtonians, I've already done the work for you. The phone number is 1-800-647-0982. For the rest of you, simply type Labor and Industries into your computer and your local government branch should pop up. Proceed from there. Ask the nice person on the other end of the line to mail you a provider application. When the application arrives it will take twenty minutes or less to fill out. Their instructions are very helpful, and there is a number provided so you may talk to a person directly if you need any additional help. Don't be embarrassed to use it if need be, it's much better for you to nitpick over every little question than to send your form out with improper information and have to wait the additional weeks to get the situation resolved. Now you are done with the forms. Great, the tough stuff is behind you. Now you get to start doing the fun stuff... treating your clients.

Wherever you live, there are benefits to becoming a provider for certain insurance companies or government programs. While the pay may take longer to arrive, the rate is fair and undivided. From a treatment perspective, it is incredibly rewarding to be able to work with your clients on an ongoing basis multiple times per week. Often you are able to get significant results with them, whereas with clients paying out of pocket and able to see you once a month you may sometimes feel you are doing nothing more than preventative care. Many of the clients you work with would never have been able to receive regular massage before. It is simply too expensive for them. The rewards of working with these clients are particularly great for me. Their whole body consciousness changes for the better. Often they become healthier and happier than before the accident. I hope that you are rewarded with this type of work as much as I have been over the years.

There are also, of course, healthcare companies that provide Massage Therapy coverage for their members. I must be honest in saying that I feel some of these companies can be misleading. There are very large insurance providers who say that their members can have 12 treatments for year, at 60, 70, or 80% coverage plus a co pay. Sounds great, right? Not so fast. This 60, 70, or 80% is based on an allotted amount that the insurance company sets. That wouldn't be so bad in theory, as you could just have a written agreement with the client that they pay the additional amount you charge. You could figure out with them how much they would owe per massage, and they would schedule massages into their budget accordingly. But unfortunately, these health insurance companies don't reveal how much their allotted amount is, ever. Not to you. Not to your client, their member. This means, for example, that after treating your client twelve times at your rate of say, $75 ($900 worth of massage therapy), the insurance will refund you for 80% of their allotted amount (we'll say $40) with a check in the amount of $384. Leaving you underpaid by $516. Worse, you and your client don't get this bad news until you have billed for the massages. So you two are stuck trying to resolve the situation fairly. I could rant about how this should not be a legal practice on the part of health insurance companies, but I won't. Instead I will arm you with this advice when dealing with them: Get all the facts, explain every detail to your client, make sure they understand how much they might have to pay out of pocket, and have your client sign a payment agreement for any money that the health insurance company doesn't pay. I discourage clients from seeing me through health insurance. After I explain why, I tell them to take their indignation to their health insurance provider and demand to have the insurance company expose it's maximum coverage amount to its members. Otherwise their so-called benefits are little more than smoke and mirrors.

I have never been one to have the patience to deal with such small details or policies I disagree with. If you are a Massage Therapist who is not averse to paperwork, however, and feels comfortable finding fair resolutions for payment with your clients (payment plans, discounted rates, etc.) there is a huge untapped market for this side of the industry. Also, if you can become a provider for these companies, I suggest you do, as it greatly increases your marketability to clients and providers such as Doctors and Chiropractors. And in the end, through patience and diligence, it can be quite rewarding. I know of one LMT, who has never been considered to have exceptional hands-on ability, she earns $120,000 a year. An estimated 70% of her clients are billed through insurance. The other 30% are hotel guests at a rate of $75 plus tips. You can do the math and quickly see she's making a lot of money dealing with those small details and disagreeable policies. These days fewer Massage Therapists are accepting health care insurance. If you feel it might be your niche market, I recommend you go for it. You would have an opportunity to tap a very large client base without a large amount of competition. You would also have a client base that is sustainable through times of economic hardship. And remember, if you are new to all this and it seems a bit daunting, it only takes a little practice before you are managing any paperwork that comes your way like a pro.

How does all this paperwork and jumping through hoops affect your bottom line? At the end of the year seeing just two out-call PIP clients each week, at an average of two treatments per week can elevate your income level by approximately $23,040 per year. If you create enough relationships with referring chiropractors, doctors, and injury lawyers you will be able to reach your goal of $100,000 per year with less than five times that amount of clients. That's just ten clients. They will typically set appointments the same time each week. It could be very easy, lucrative and rewarding work for you if you are so inspired. Combining higher-education massage modalities with out call and injury treatment can keep your body free from repetitive stress injuries as well as your piggy bank full. Just remember the golden rule of marketing: When you are the busiest, you should be marketing the most. It means that a slow time is just around the corner. Don't let your ten clients all stop getting treatment at the same time and then start marketing to find another ten. Market the entire time so that when a client ceases to get treatment, another easily replaces them. This is the secret to being prosperous as a Massage Therapist, whatever medium you choose to work within.

Marketing for PIP and L&I must be looked at like marketing for niche market. Rather than casting a wide advertising net and "catching" every client under the sun, find ways to be very precise in the advertising to this particular client demographic. You do this by researching the statistics provided through the U.S. Department of Labor Bureau of statistics, for example. A quick glance at their charts comparing white collar worker neurotic injuries versus blue collar worker injuries shows that 64 of every 100 white collar workers take days off from work due to neurotic reactions to stress, and only 20 of every 100 do so for injuries and illnesses. Blue collar workers on the other hand, have the opposite statistics. 62 of 100 blue collar take time off from work due to illness or injury. Only 24 of them take a leave due to neurotic reactions to stress. This statistic alone, tells you a lot about which group of people should be marketed to for traumatic injuries to the body. According the U.S Dept. of Labor – " Of the 5.8 million cases of work related illnesses and injuries that resulted in either lost work time, medical treatment, restriction of work, or transfer to another job 281,128 were disorders associated with repeated trauma (with 29,937 cases of carpel tunnel syndrome). That is a lot of people in the U.S. that needs a good dose of Cross Fiber Friction Massage! Many of these people don't know that Massage Therapy can reduce or completely remove these symptoms. Many of them resort to surgery. It is our responsibility to educate them on alternative methods that can help them before such a drastic step is taken. In my opinion all options should be exhausted before invasive surgery. The way that we educate the public is through our advertisements and marketing campaigns. Self promotion has been given a bad rap by many Massage Therapists, but it is the most effective way to get your message into the world, and those that embrace it as a marketing technique often flourish. Whether you take the "controversial" route (like I have done for this book) or the "safe" route (which is recommended), you must self promote in one way or another to get a number of clients that is satisfactory to earning a living wage in this profession.

The top three most effective ways to advertise to PIP and L&I clients is to educate your direct referrals, develop question-affirmation based advertisements that attract your demographic, and to educate through your website by filling it with keyword phrases that people researching their insurance benefits will type into Google. You can find these most used phrases at www.googlekeywords.com. Enlist every MD, Chiropractor, Personal Trainer, Injury Lawyer, Acupuncturist, and Rehabilitation Specialist within a ten -mile radius of your clinic about your enthusiasm for Injury Treatment Massage. Educate them on how and why Cross Fiber Friction can diminish scar tissue built up in the metacarpals, ease their patients' pain, and remove the need for surgery. Educate them on Massage as treatment for whiplash, thoracic outlet syndrome, tennis elbow, post-operation scars tissue reduction, and more. Once their patients come back with glowing reviews, you'll be sent patients for a lifetime. (But remember to always say "thank you" in a way that they understand and appreciate, every one's idea of graciousness is different.) Putting together a brochure of all the information you would like to share with these professionals is highly recommended. It gives your entire presentation a professional boost. Your paper advertisements that you put into the world should always generate an enthusiastic "Yes!" from your target market. Headlines such as "Have you been injured on the job? Did you know you may qualify to receive Massage Therapy as treatment and have it covered by your Worker's Compensation Plan?" Or "have you been in an auto accident? Did you know injuries may arise as much as six months after the initial collision? Massage Therapy can alleviate and even prevent these injuries. Your auto insurance will likely cover massage multiple times per week with a prescription. Make sure you call your doctor and your Massage Therapist today." These types of phrases are compelling for someone who has been recently injured and needs treatment. These phrases ask them the question that gets their attention and then provides them a solution to that question. This provides them with a feeling of safety and trust in your services, even before they meet you. Find publications in your region that cater to the demographic you are marketing to. There are websites that cater to unionized employees such as www.unitedworkforce.org. You can pay around $250 per year to be one of three Massage Therapists who advertise through them in your county. Opportunities are opening up all around us to educate the blue collar demographic about massage and its benefits, if only you seek them out. Both of the above mentioned tag lines are great starting points for you to come up with messages that captivate, educate, and sympathize with your niche market. However taglines are meaningless without an ad that generates trust from the people you are marketing to. The blue collar market that you are trying to appeal to has different set of needs and likes than the luxury market. There is a smaller percentage of this group seeking Massage Treatment. Many have a limited understanding of it. Your best trust inspiring ads toward this demographic will be educational, medical based, and will have little flowery prose. For the most part, your ads should be of meat and potato variety. Clean lines, basic colors, traditional fonts, and clear language should be the base of these ads. If you are marketing in a certain publication that uses specific catch phrases, use them if you're able. If your Massage business is named something flowery or new-agey, it may be best to market to this group with your name and credentials instead of your business name. While it sounds like I'm generalizing people's needs, I am merely speaking of the statistical nature of different groups of people. It's not only good business to understand how to effectively market to different types of people it develops excellent communication skills. Effective advertising to any demographic shows a level of respect for those that need your care. Once they feel that respect, you will have the opportunity to educate them about their injuries and get down to the business of treating them.

Working with clients who have been injured is a wonderful way to create life-long relationships with your clients. Once you have established the trust that comes with helping someone heal from a traumatic injury, they usually never think to see another Massage Therapist again. You, in turn get to witness the changes that occur in your clients with regular massage. This is a wonderful affirmation of what we give to the world. It is a very good thing.

"There is no point at which you can say, 'Well, I'm successful now. I might as well take a nap.'"

- Carrie Fisher

10

EARN INCOME WHILE *YOU* RELAX

The final ways in which you can significantly increase your level of income without increasing your workload is to contract services to other Massage Therapists and/or to offer a product line for retail sale. We'll first discuss the option of contracting services, as this is a natural option for anyone with a successful Massage Therapy business. Once you have successfully built a solid client base, your advertising efforts will continue to bring you new clients. You worked hard for that potential client and it would be unwise to simply refuse service to them and lose all potential income by turning them away.

To contract Massage Therapists you must have them first sign a contract stating that you are not legally responsible to them in any way, that they are an independent contractor. This means that they are responsible for keeping track of their own finances and tax obligations and they can be "let go" for any reason without legal recourse. There are benefits for both parties in this arrangement. You get to refer your overflow appointments and keep anywhere from 50% of the cost of massage. You also have an opportunity to build your business based on excellent availability, as there is always someone available when you have a list of contractors working with you. And you experience the rewards of helping Massage Therapists in the industry who can use additional income.

The contracting MTs are grateful for this arrangement because they can accept or refuse any massage you offer them. They aren't tied down to a specific schedule. Also, the rate of pay is generally higher than a spa or medical office pays. I typically pay between $40 and $60 per hour depending on the treatment and location. This higher level of compensation keeps the best quality therapists working for my company. And many Massage Therapists feel overwhelmed at the thought of having to generate their own business (similar to how you may have felt before reading this book). These MTs won't bat an eyelash at the percentage you're keeping. They'll be so grateful that you did all the "business-y stuff" for them.

You do not have to be a huge success before you start contracting other Massage Therapists. All you need is an overflow of business. If you have had to turn away one client, you have a reason to refer business. Refusing to see clients because of scheduling restrictions is like flushing money down the toilet. If you don't have the high level of requests that warrant you to contract a fleet of Massage Therapists yet, at the very least form a community of trusted Massage Therapists who provide incentive to refer back and forth. Perhaps you provide each other monetary incentive, new client referrals or trade for bodywork.

Many Massage Therapists express dismay at the idea of referring their clients to others. They see it as a potential to lose that client. My thoughts on this are: 1) if your client decides to continue seeing another MT, you were eventually going to lose them as a client anyway. 2) If a client found someone a better fit, most likely they weren't a perfect fit for you, either. Their leaving will open up a time slot in your schedule for a client who is head over heels for your style of bodywork. 3) Some clients like variety in their bodywork practitioners. Often, the client will return to seeing you.

The point is that the tighter you hang on to your clients, the more you restrict their healing process, and your own company's growth. Clients have a way of coming in and out of your life. If you depend on your income from them, you will find yourself in a financial pickle much of the time. Focusing on your current clients as if they were "yours" rather than focusing on marketing and referring outside of yourself will only keep you marginally successful and working far too many hours to stay healthy.

I know that referring business initially feels like you have to be someone's "boss". I remember how it felt for me the first time I went looking for LMTs to contract for my little company. I didn't measure up to a "successful business owner" in my mind. But I did have an overflow of business, and it made me very uncomfortable to say "no" to potential income. As a result, I was working ridiculous amounts of hours. One day it just "clicked". I didn't need to be a huge company, or to be a "big business woman" to contract services. I didn't need to be anyone's "boss". I just needed what I already had: too many clients. And I needed to refer them out and get paid for my efforts. If you follow my advice, you will soon have an overflow of business that requires you to refer some out. The best part about this is that eventually you will get to pare back on your own twenty-hour workweek, and still make $100,000 by the year's end!

Another great way to be able to work less, work hours that are more favorable to you, and earn more, is to sell a product line that is easily incorporated into your clientele's health and wellness regime. Whether you provide massage that is sports treatment-oriented, health and wellness-centered, or provide relaxing spa treatments, there is always a consumer need for products that the client can use at home enhance their health and beauty. I've searched high and low for a line of products that were of the highest organic quality combined with an easy, low entry cost for sellers and an impressive company philosophy. I believe I have found that in Miessence: a product line that stands in a class of its own as the first and only comprehensive range of certified organic skin, hair, cosmetics and body care products on the planet. Wait until you see the extensive selection of organic ingredients in this line. These unique and unrivalled products are the only intelligent choice for quality and purity of ingredients, integrity of claims and freshness and potency of product. On top of all that, Miessence products carry a "100% Money-back guarantee" so your clients and their family members are sure to be pleased 100% of the time with their purchases. You can sign up to be a member through me at www.hundredthousanddollarmassage.com. Just look for the Miessence home page link. There I will explain, in detail how you can get started selling this product line that will not only have a positive effect on the well being of others and the world, but might possibly increase your yearly earnings greatly.

Even if you think you don't enjoy being a "sales person", it's easy to sell a product line that you love and your client is already looking to buy. Just as you should always offer an increase in massage length to any client who needs or wants it, you should feel equally as comfortable offering the client the ability to buy the massage lotion, mud wrap, aromatherapy oil or body brush that you just used for their treatment. Once you build a close bond with your clients, they will reveal insecurities about their weight, cellulite, blemishes, dull hair and skin. You will have a solution to offer them that is of the highest quality. They will be able to pay for the item the very same day of the complaint and feel relieved that someone they know and trust recommended it to them. But, remember that it is outside of your scope of practice to diagnose people. Resist the urge to do so. And don't forget that any no's you hear along the way is not "no" to you, only to what you are offering. So keep trying to enhance your clients' lives until you hear a yes. Don't stop until the sales are rolling in without effort.

And finally, the proof is in the pudding, as they say. So for any doubters that still don't believe you can work few hours per week and bring in $100,000 per year (a year is considered 11 months in these estimates, figuring in one month for vacation), let me break it down for you:

80 Out-call PIP or L&I appointments per month
(10 clients treated twice per week)
$125 average cost of treatment
Grand total = $110,000 per year

48 VIP Out-call massage clients per month

$200 average cost of 90 min. appt. plus $20 gratuity

Grand total = 105,600

*Consider that rates for out-call massages increase in the mornings (typically before 9 Am) and the evenings (typically after 8:30 pm). The cost is typically an additional 25% of the listed massage price. Being an early bird or a night owl can significantly increase your income in this industry.

48 Outcall PIP or L&I appointments per month ($125 per session)

+ 10 outcall massages per month ($200 per 90 min. session)

+ Contracting 35 LMT ($50 per referral)

Grand total = $107,250

80 in-studio Specialty Massages or L&I injury treatment per month ($85 per session)

+ Contracting 46 MTs per month ($50 per referral)

Grand Total = $100,100

Adding a product line's generated income, such as Miessence, could add an additional $0 to $1,000,000 per year. The earning potential is based on your passion and willingness to succeed.

Don't think these numbers are being pulled from thin air. This is standard in Seattle, Washington for those who provide luxury services, travel massage or injury treatment massage. I've been earning more than this hourly rate of pay for quite a few years. I have mixed injury work, prenatal massage and a variety of other modalities out of my home office with outcall massage given to trusted clients in their homes and at high-end hotels. I underestimated tips here, as well, since people generally tip closer to 20%. You do the math. In many cities, the rates for outcall massage will be much higher. Some cities and many suburbs and small towns the rate will be lower. But your living expenses will be more or less there too.

This brings me to this final point about income level: How much is enough? Do you really need to bring in $100,000 per year? Or would you feel like a success earning $80,000 $60,000 or

$40,000 and having significant amounts of free time for hobbies, family and friends. Our society is very money focused. But I personally believe that everyone has a set of values within that includes more than just money to be happy.

The year I wrote this book, I didn't aim to make money. My goal was to live comfortably and finish the book. I did both. I didn't hit the $100,000 mark, but I brought in enough that I lived well above the national average. And truthfully, any year I brought in $60,000 gross, doing something as profound as healing people, something that I, in fact, love doing.... I felt like the luckiest lady alive. Perhaps we should start listening to the advice of Sages and Saints. Maybe what we need is to do something we love each and every day, and the money will follow. In the words of Confucius, "Choose a job that you love, and you will never have to work a day in your life." And in my own words, "Choose a job you love that pays very well, you'll never work a day in your life, and you'll make BANK!"

And remember, there is a world of possibilities in the profession of Massage Therapy. Once you are working for yourself and marketing your business with excellence, you can bring in a great living providing massage in vast amount of locations. Seated massage is a great way to expand your company and contract other Massage Therapists. Many companies, hospitals, athletic events, and assisted living homes are eager to have one or more MTs massage groups of people on a regular schedule. Everywhere you look there are opportunities for building yourself a successful practice. You need only be motivated, confident, and eager to teach people about the amazing benefits of massage. And as I said before, if you become specialized at treating any conditions, you need only advertise to the groups of clients who get these conditions most. Golfers, basketball players, runners, computer techs, they each have specific symptoms from working at their trades or hobbies repetitively. You could be the one Massage Therapist in your town known for having the "magic touch" for any of these folks. Secrets of success are only as good as your desire and drive to succeed.

"Empty pockets never held anyone back. Only empty heads and empty hearts can do that. "

- Norman Vincent Peale

11

THINK OUTSIDE THE BOX

Some of the best opportunities that come your way are missed for one reason. Your mind is shut (so is mine quite often, it is the human condition). Just like it may never have occurred to you that a slightly "off" schedule could result in a doubled yearly income, countless opportunities for greater success are offered to you every day. All it requires is tweaking your mind just a tad bit off-center to see these opportunities. There are critics who claim: "Everything in the world has been done." I challenge this statement. Every day new technologies and business models are created that open up a whole new world of opportunity for Massage Therapists, if only they find them and create them. All it takes initially is a willingness to open your mind, assume a positive thought pattern about the possibilities available to you, and a willingness to try new things, despite criticisms from those who wish to remain stagnant in their old fear paradigms. The criticisms will come, but once you reap the rewards of creating in this world, and ushering forth innovation, you will be fulfilled and challenged in ways they may never know. And there will always be people who embrace new thoughts and ideas. These people will step forward to offer assistance when you need it. But the only validation you must rely on comes from within you. It is, ultimately, not your business what others think of you. It is your business to follow your heart and mind.

My spa began because I uncovered an untapped opportunity and refused to pass it up. This opportunity was available to many Massage Therapists in my area, yet none of them saw it. I did and I jumped on it. I jumped on a plan to expand my business by fulfilling a current need that had been left unacknowledged, with a zero dollar budget. What I have learned from this is invaluable and I hope that my sharing will encourage you to see opportunities all around you. Many such opportunities are everywhere.

Before the creation of Umi, I was a sole proprietor and an independent contractor. I had a home office in a neighborhood on the edge of the city. I also supplemented my income with hotel work and travel massage. My schedule was packed and my phone was ringing off the hook. I was ecstatic, but knew that my client load was unsustainable in the long run. Because of the nature of out-of-town clients needing to schedule last-minute massages, I had been required to "jump" for too many years to sustain my level of income. It was time to evolve so that a burnout wouldn't hit me a second time in my career. So by observing what needs were present in my current contracting positions, I began to form a plan to fulfill those needs.

The first need I uncovered while providing in-room hotel massage was an agreement of consistent standards. Whenever I gave couples massage with other Massage Therapists, I often witnessed disjointed and inconsistent customer service in the guest rooms. There were zero standards involving room setup, billing and paperwork, policies, problem resolution etc. This left some of the clients visibly confused, and me, admittedly, ashamed. I didn't like working in-room with Massage Therapists who didn't embody basic standards and integrity with the hotel guests. These guests were paying a premium and I felt they deserved service that reflected the luxury prices.

The second need I observed was the need for excellent contracted Licensed Massage Therapists to be the first choice to work with the hotels' guests. I noticed that while my reputation earned me a spot at the top of the call list in these hotels, many gifted and honest MTs had mostly flown under the radar. In fact, there seemed to be more reward going to Massage Therapists who were versed in bribing and schmoozing concierges, than in customer service. For whatever reason, these other tried and true Massage Therapists hadn't been able to earn a spot anywhere near the top of the list. But these were the individuals with whom I wanted to work in-room, to not only enhance my own reputation, but to ensure that a professional atmosphere would be maintained and to increase repeat business through client trust.

I realized that this was never going to happen unless I made it happen. So I took the bull by the horns. I contacted all the independent contractors who I knew were excellent and honest, but hungry, and offered to supply them with business for a 0% -30%

referral fee, depending on the location and type of massage given. Not a single one refused. I asked for a copy of a major hotel's independent contractor contracts, changed and deleted anything that didn't apply to my company and had a lawyer sign off on it as legally usable for my own contractual agreement. I then proceeded to present my idea to the hotel concierge who knew of my reputation (I was known for upholding and encouraging development of professional standards in the industry as well as having excellent client feedback and the highest number of requests, as well as being the favored LMT among visiting celebrities). I assured them that if they chose to use Spa Umi, I would not only make their jobs easier (by making their phone calls for them) but that quality service would be overseen by myself and only the best Licensed Massage Therapists would be referred business.

This last part was the key to success. While many other Massage Therapists were trying to outdo one another with higher tips for the concierges, I cornered the market by offering them convenience. Concierges are busy people. At any given moment, they may be handling three calls and a list of requests. Calling down a list of Massage Therapists to find the one that is available is time-consuming. Many of them simply didn't have the time and considered these phone calls a burden. I took that burden off their hands. As a result, Spa Umi rewarded some of the best Massage Therapists in Seattle. I was able to work with a hand-selected group of people whose skill and integrity I admired, and I was the first call, every time. This allowed me a freedom in my schedule that I previously didn't have. Also, I never needed to turn a massage away (which is my preferred mode of operation). And finally, because I was the first call from these busy hotels, I was able to design my schedule however I saw fit, allowing me to maintain my reputation of excellent availability, while granting me some much-needed freedom.

My idea was a success. In just six months after opening, Umi received requests from four major hotels to be their sole provider company. We were the first mobile spa to be approached for this type of account in the Seattle-Bellevue area. It took implementing impressive standards, and only working with the most disciplined Massage Therapists, to make this happen, but it did happen in record time. I opted out, in order to maintain the integrity of the company by staying small, but I learned everything I needed to learn throughout its development. I learned that one could build a business on the cheap, and take care of fellow MTs, by uncovering opportunities that have been within reach all along. Better still, once I had mastered running the Spa in the hotels, I expanded into working with established companies providing corporate massage events. These proved to be very lucrative, and typically provided the contracting Massage Therapists weeks of advanced notice before the scheduled event. Those Massage Therapists who couldn't "jump" for the VIPS were still provided for. It was a perfect arrangement for everyone involved.

There are people, corporations, clinics and professionals everywhere whose clientele and staff benefit from massage services. Some of them need you to educate, or help them uncover those needs. Some of them need you to increase their profit or efficiency in their current utilization of these services. Most of them don't realize that they have an unfulfilled need that you can fulfill – until you make them aware of it and offer a resolution.

Until I approached the concierges and pointed out to them that I could lighten their workload and increase the standards of customer service given to their clientele, at no charge to them, they never knew the need existed. Calling down a long list of Massage Therapists was a part of their job description. It never occurred to them that there was a way to get someone else to do it faster and more effectively, until I offered them a better way.

Many people will say that business is for the corrupt and greedy, making money is evil, and starting a business costs a bucket full of cash. I challenge those beliefs too. Sometimes, all one needs is a desire to increase standards of current conditions. If you are a person who constantly seeks new and better ways of being in the world, a profitable idea is circulating through your mind, right now. Jump on it. What are you waiting for? Every day I see opportunities that Massage Therapists haven't snagged. I can't ride the Washington ferry system or shop at the local organic foods market without asking myself: "Why hasn't someone set up a seated massage business here?" Just the other day I brainstormed the idea of creating packages of three (trimester) or nine (full term) massages to offer on baby registries. Allowing anyone the ability to contribute any amount of money to the package. As a result, families and friends would be able to give a high-cost, much-appreciated gift to the mommy-to-be, despite different financial situations. (And the MT is focusing efforts on large packages versus one client at a time, which is a much more effective marketing strategy.) I'm surprised opportunities like these haven't been embraced and realized yet. The point is, there are new ways of being in this profession everywhere one looks.

Whether in an upswing or a depressed economy, we can continue to elevate our earning potential with vision and determination. In fact, even times of lagging economic growth are perfect to educate people on the statistics of stress, how it kills, and how to decrease its symptoms and manifestations through massage. Many people don't know that their insurance covers a portion of massage. Again, each and every day I think: "Why aren't more Massage Therapists educating people of their insurance coverage benefits and massage's ability to reduce stress, in their current advertisements?" (This type of advertisement also benefits greatly from a bold headline that asks an affirmative response from the potential client.)

Wherever you are, whatever you are doing, stop and look around, just for a moment. Ask yourself: how can Massage Therapy be introduced into your daily life? How can it begin to be considered a necessity and part of a balanced daily life, versus a luxury? What is your contribution to that movement? We already understand it to be a necessity, now it's time to educate others in our communities. If we all join together in this conversation and willingness to move forward, eventually any one of us will be able to easily create a work-life that is lucrative, rewarding, exhilarating and full of joy. Now is the time to move forward. Not tomorrow. Today. I'll see you outside of the box.

"I'd like to live as a poor man with lots of money."

- Pablo Picasso

12

SAVE MONEY TO MAKE MONEY

You may have noticed that I push ways of saving money throughout this book. Whether it's suggestions of buying used, or less expensive, products on eBay or Craigslist, or taking advantage of tax write-offs, I believe that one of the ways in which Massage Therapists make money is by saving money.

While the first half of my career was a struggle, being broke during that time actually became an advantage later in life. Just as Spa Umi began as a creative way of cornering a market with very little start-up budget, my penny-pinching has continued to benefit my business choices and my lifestyle. Money is no use to you if you are giving half of it to the government or spending your entire profit margin on business expenses that don't benefit your lifestyle as a whole. Being broke, in the early days, made it necessary for me to uncover ways of being alternately frugal and spendthrift. The places that I placed my money were often counterintuitive to my peers and friends. Even successful business owners of larger companies often scratched their heads at why I would continue to rent, or drive a basic vehicle, for example, when my business was at its peak. I was, after all, financially able to drive a luxury vehicle and buy a dream home. But all of it was carefully measured in my mind, and as a result I was able to have excess spending money for the things that I loved.

There was always money in the budget for dining out, the arts, designer clothing, and travel. These are my weaknesses. But to ensure that I had this extra money coming in, I made choices that literally made friends laugh out loud. For example, I drove a used 2-door 2000 Honda Civic EX for five years. In fact, I still would be driving it today, had I not relocated out of the country for a year. I used this car as my business vehicle. Before I purchased this particular car, I researched its reliability, gas mileage, and depreciation through the annual Consumer Reports Used Car Guide. I read through countless graphs and reports, weighed all the factors and finally decided this particular vehicle was the best choice for increasing my income in the long term. This car was tiny, gas-efficient, yet sturdy and safe. The trunk was ample enough for a massage table and supplies. The price was only $10,000. The depreciation was nearly non-existent. (Apparently this vehicle was huge among teenagers in foreign countries, so it always retained its value.) Here I was, rocking designer shoes and handbags and driving a two-door Civic. My ex-boyfriend would laugh daily. I often heard: "That car doesn't suit your image. You wear designer clothes and drive a basic vehicle. When will you buy a new one?" My reply was always: "When this one dies, I guess. This car does suit me. I am very practical at my core. You and I just share different ideas of where our money should be placed. I believe that clothing is part of my marketing budget and that my automobile should earn me money, not lose me money." I drove that little wind-up toy car for five years. When I sold it, the new owner paid $1,500 less than I had paid for it half-a-decade previously. I made hundreds of thousands of dollars through my travel massage business in that car. I never regretted a moment of making the choice to not bog myself down in payments to keep up with my friends' beliefs that I needed a luxury vehicle to maintain my image.

During this time I lived in a gorgeous five-bedroom turn of the century house. It boasted floor to ceiling windows with views of Lake Union and the city. I chose to rent this house versus buy elsewhere. My rental cost was $1,700 a month. My friends would balk at my rental payment. "Why don't you BUY something?" they would ask. EVERYONE was buying. Renting was not for people earning a decent living, they said. But my logic was that it was more advantageous for me to rent a large house and turn an entire floor of it into a massage space/office, than to take a risk of buying into a market that I felt was bloated and uncertain. My $1,700 going towards a mortgage wouldn't have afforded me any more than a one-bedroom condo. And a massage space would have needed to be rented elsewhere, simultaneously. Thus my cost of living and business would have been greatly increased at the end of each year, with no guarantee of return on the condo. However, renting that large house in a prime neighborhood with a professional office and studio, ample parking, and easy access to the freeway, turned out to be very profitable. At the end of each year, at tax time, I would be allowed to write off one third of my rent and utilities. The floor I used for business had its own bathroom, an outside door, and was a clear and indisputable write-off. As a result, I was able to live in a luxury house, with three bedrooms all to myself, for the cost equivalent of a studio apartment in a bad neighborhood. I tried to explain my logic to friends and associates, but it wasn't until the housing market declined that they finally understood why I had chosen to rent all those years. I was earning money through that property in a manner that I knew to be a sure thing: my business. My business's profit was something I could control and guarantee. The housing market was something that was out of my control. While many people thought I was being irresponsible, it turned out I was actually doing the opposite.

I have never been a gambler. And while many people will tell you that having your own business is a gamble, I strongly disagree. Once I began to realize that having your own business is really the only guarantee of employment, I began to question societal agreements about automobile and home financing and tax write-offs. And these questions led me to seek out ways of being in the world that were of benefit to my pocketbook, despite those choices seeming counter-intuitive to the cultural agreement of the time.

There are, of course, many other beneficial tax write-offs. Many Massage Therapists will write their vacations off, for example. They do this by educating themselves in a modality that is only offered in a particular country. They will attend the class for its entire duration, and pad either end of the trip with the number of non-educational days that the IRS allows. The laws change what is allowed periodically, so one must stay updated on changes. But I have known more than one MT who has traveled to Hawaii for Lomi Lomi training, and padded their two-week trip with two "vacation days" before the class begins and two days after the class ends. As a result, they were able to write the entire trip off. Meaning, they didn't have to give that money to the government in taxes, because they had spent that money on a business expense. It's not risky to take advantage of the benefits that the IRS offers you. It's good sense.

I always take advantage of the opportunity to write off the maximum amount for donations to charity each year. Rather than just donating "stuff" to goodwill, I make an effort to get involved in the community and give donations of services and money. The rewards of sharing with people in need are even greater than the advantages of being able to write the donation off at the end of the year. But it is really wonderful that the government allows us to have that opportunity.

You can check out the rating of any non-profit organization at www.charitynavigator.org. Their ratings will reveal to you how efficient and organized your charity of choice is, how much the charity's CEO is keeping as salary each year, and what portion of your donation goes to the cause versus the marketing costs. It's a wonderful site and extremely eye-opening. Some wonderful causes are being under-funded, while many intensely advertised or currently "hip" causes are bloated beyond reason with funding. This site will put your fears to rest about whether or not your donation is going to a worthy cause.

Massage Therapists often express fear about starting up their own business because of the fear of taxation. Many defend their belief that the IRS will keep 50% of their earnings at the end of the year. While each country is different in its taxation structure, and each year the rules may slightly change, my life in the U.S. is built around tax write-offs. When I spend money, I look for the ways in which that money will bring reward back to my business. If it doesn't, I ask myself if it is REALLY worth the immediate gratification. If it's not, I can't justify the purchase. I urge you to meet with an accountant and have clear and indisputable tax write-offs defined for your business. For when you are a business owner, your business is your life. Your spending reflects that. The government has provided you with many ways not to be taxed on those efforts. All you need to do is educate yourself on those write-offs and take advantage of them. It's why they are there.

Contrary to popular belief, people at the IRS office are quite nice. I've chatted with them a few times. The IRS can offer you payment plans, and sometimes extensions on your amounts due. If you are proactive with them, they will find a solution with you if necessary. The problem, as I see it, is that there is this fear of auditing that surpasses the fear of death or bodily injury for many people. I once panicked at the thought of being responsible for business taxes. I imagined the "big bad wolf of the IRS" hunting me down, catching a decimal point mistake, and punishing me by locking me in a cold, hard dungeon and slapping me with a fine so large I would never be able to pay it back. Not ever in a million years.

There are thousands of versions of these overly-dramatic fear scenarios going through people's minds about the IRS. In truth, your taxes are the last thing that should be keeping you from building your own business. Once you understand how to structure your life around tax write-offs, it often feels like the government rewards small business owners. But it is one's responsibility to research and follow the laws to the last letter to enjoy those benefits without fear. It can and is done every day, by business owners around the globe. Many of them were once scared of the IRS at some point too. But they pushed through that fear to follow their passions and reap the rewards. Don't let an unwarranted fear of the IRS hold you back from the best way to earn a livable wage in this profession. Take a look at how your life is structured. Are you currently spending your money on business and lifestyle needs that work for you? Or is your spending working against you? Once you step back and look at your budget, you may be shocked to discover that a lot of money is going to unnecessary expenditures, while many of the necessities such as effective marketing, and personal image are being neglected. Avoid nickel and diming yourself by purchasing massage "stuff" that the client cares nothing about, in an effort to make yourself feel that you are taking advantage of tax write-offs. Unnecessary spending is unnecessary, no matter how you justify it. Likewise, if you understand that spending more in an area will increase your profit margin and lifestyle (such as a home office) by all means spend more, despite the protest you may hear from people who are not as educated about the nature of your business. After all, it is your business. Only you see the books. Only you know where the benefits lie, and how to best reap the rewards of your choices. Spending wisely will allow you to live a life of luxury and security, even before you hit the $100,000 per year mark. Set up a massage trade with an accountant today. Start redefining your financial goals and spending habits. Once you start saving money while living a better life, you'll be happy you did.

"Always dream and shoot higher than you know you can do. Don't bother just to be better than your contemporaries or predecessors. Try to be better than yourself."

- William Faulkner

13

AIM HIGHER THAN YOU DREAM

Have I said before that I want for you to be happy, healthy, and prosperous in this profession? Well, then I have said it again. If you ask me, it's about time that people who take the high road to success reach it. As I said before, we need our healers, teachers, mentors, and saints to live full and prosperous lives. Your aiming toward that goal will put us one more person closer to that goal. You aiming to be your best and brightest self will serve as an example for anyone who ever doubted that the healers of this world can be prosperous.

Marian Williamson once said, "Our deepest fear is not that we are inadequate. Our deepest fear is that we are powerful beyond measure. Our playing small does not serve the world." For many years, I played small. I believed money to be a necessary evil. Now I understand that with money, I can bring positive change into the world. Then I believed that I couldn't achieve anything more than moderate success through backbreaking hard work. Now I know that if I reach for higher success than has been previously achieved, I may just reach it easier than expected. Those days I listened to people who would exclaim that my dreams and ambitions were not possible. Now I only listen to those who have reached similarly "impossible" heights. I previously felt helplessness and despair as I watched the world's tragedies unfold. Terrible atrocities inflicted on humans and our environment: child slavery and oppression, factory farming, deforestation, species extinction, war, poverty, hate crimes, abuses of power and global destruction. I felt overwhelmed with knowledge, and paralyzed by thoughts of uselessness. Now I believe that by making myself a bigger player in this world, I will have more ability to help the world's inhabitants.

I once asked the CEO of a major corporation how a little person like me could change the world. I said that I was beginning to believe that I couldn't, in fact. His reply was unexpected, and deeply affected me. I have never seen the world, or my place in it, the same way since. He said, "You know, Meagan, there are others of us who once felt the same way as you, ineffectual and overwhelmed by the world's atrocities, and we decided that the only real way to beat the bad guys at their game was to play in their court. We put on suits, started in the mailroom, held our idealistic tongues and worked our way up until we own the better share of the company. Once you are at the top of a company, whether it be a corporation, or your own homegrown business, you are able to influence people on a larger scale." He urged me to stop playing small with my life and to stop assuming that everyone at the top was greedy and corrupt. To imagine the good I could create in the world if I had more influence. I will never forget this man. This "surfer in a suit" as he described himself, plugging his way up the ladder, keeping his beliefs mum until the day when he could say, "Well boys, a new boss is in town, and I've got some ideas...".

His story illuminated a path that had been in front of me all along. One that I believe is laid out for each of us: a path to greatness, one that leads to dream fulfillment and ends with a look back on life with a feeling of accomplishment. I know now that I can help heal the world, not by playing small, but by being bigger in the game of life than I previously thought possible. And so can you.

Look around you. People accomplish the impossible every day with less than you. I have revealed to you a few of my struggles. A less-than-perfect childhood, chronic pain, brain damage, poverty, illness, and so many more obstacles than you will ever know. But aren't there obstacles for all of us? Don't we all have insecurities, setbacks, and perceived weaknesses to overcome? Of course we do. This is what it is to be human. The key is in recognizing how you can play upon your strengths and your perceived weaknesses.

I know of a personal trainer who has been blind since early childhood. Not only has he pushed himself beyond limitations others have placed upon him, he has turned this difference into a strength. He has discovered his blindness is an advantage when working with women with eating disorders. Because he is blind, these women are able to trust him. They are not focused on whether he is judging their bodies or not. As a result he is able to guide his clients towards a goal of health and fitness much faster.

What separates the extraordinary humans the average was summed up by MC Escher perfectly when he said, "Only those who attempt the absurd will achieve the impossible." So get out there.

Attempt. Achieve. Live your dreams. I have laid out a very effective plan for you to follow on the beginning of your journey, one that will allow you to heal people, work few hours, and make great money. This should leave you with plenty of resources and time to begin seeing the world and your dreams in a new light and begin making your dreams a reality.

I urge you to change the way you see the world, what it holds for you, what you will give back in return. Consider that if only 20% of the people hold 80% of the world's wealth at any given time, that 80% should be in the hands of caring individuals who want to change the world for the better. Individuals like you. Set that goal that seems impossible. So that every time an obstacle arises you will remain excited, and move mountains to achieve it. Whether you want to build schools for children around the globe, be on the Oprah show, raise $1,000,000.00 for Darfur's orphans, put $500,000 into your retirement fund in less than ten years, or simply be the happiest Massage Therapist on earth: chase that dream. Don't stop until the "impossible" is yours.

"You have a unique gift to offer this world. Each and every person that you come in contact with, you affect in a way that cannot be measured, and its effect is immediate and infinite. You have chosen to place yourself in a position of contributing positively to the world through your clients. The gifts, relationships, and knowledge that you will receive from making such a choice will be overwhelming at times. Any obstacles that you have to overcome to reap the benefits will be well worth it. This is your journey. Listen to the small, still voice within and fight any opposition with the fierceness of a warrior. This is your birthright. Do not let anyone deter you from it. You are the true healers. Stand tall. Assert yourself. Believe in yourself. Demand that your dreams come true. Let no one get in your way. Kill those that try with kindness. And finally, get out of your own way so that you may watch your dreams take shape and manifest right before your very eyes."

~ Meagan

INDEX

P [185]
Hourly rate of pay, P [222]
Hours of operation, P [134,142]
Human body, P [49,65]
Hydrotherapy, P [197]
Hygiene, P 110,114,115,116]
Hypersensitivity, P [34]
Hyper tense, P [55]
Hypnotherapy, P [38]
Hypnotic spell, P [145]
Hypnotists, P [145]
Hypoallergenic, P [77]

I
Image, P[98,102,104,118,122,123,125,127,130,133,161,164,182,247]
Inappropriate advances, P [178]
Inflammation, P [37,195]
Initial attraction, P [131]
Injury, P[9,37,50,92,132,141,193,194,197,198,206,209,221,222,245]
lawyers, P [132,141,206]
treatment modalities, P [197]
Integrity, P [27,58,171,173,218,228,231,232]
Intelligent advertisement, P [143]
Internal structures, P [61]

Internet, P [135,136,200]
high-speed, P [135,136]
Intuition, P[5,22,25,45,46,47,48,49,55,59,80]
Intuitive, P[7,32,43,45,46,47,48,50,51,54,80,94,239,243]
Invoice, P [168]
iPod or CDs, P [183]
Iridology, P [38]
Isaac Bashevis Singer, P [97]

J
Jerks, P [174]
Joints, P [36,37,61]
Journey to success, P [118]
Judge, P[91,98,109,118,158,181,182,183]
Junk-free diet, P [112]

K
Keywords, P [127,135,209]
Knot, P [50,53,55,57]

L
Labor and Industries (L&I), P [92,200,201]
Last-minute appointments, P [111]
Licensed Massage Therapist P[10,17,28,41,45,85,116,118,122,170,229,230]
Licensing, P [76,168]
Lifestyle,

Nerve, P [61,80]
NFL player, P [109]

Niche, P
[7,49,58,98,135,159,187,205,
207,211]
    market, P
[58,98,135,187,205,207,211]
Non-invasive draping, P [93]
Non-Newtonian experiment,
P [7,62,63]
North American consumer, P
[148]
NPI (National Provider
    Identification), P [200]

O
Offensive odors, P [113]
Oil, P
[8.75,77,78,108,113,118,216,
219]
One-stop shopping, P [87]
Ooblec, P [63,64]
Opportunity, P
[10,38,55,68,91,146,160,205,
212,215,226,227,243,244]
Oprah, P
[44,100,101,105,254]
Optimal results, P [92]
Organic, P
[111,112,113,218,233]
    co-ops, P [112]
free range, and locally
grown, P [112]
Organization, P [3,88,244]
Organs, P [61]
Out-call clients, P [183]
Outdated equipment, P [139]
Outside the box,

P [9,138,146,226]

P
Pact of honor, P [171]
Pain, P
[7,15,21,22,25,26,28,30,33,3
4,35,38,40,41,45,50,51,54,56,
57,58,74,88,89,115,154,184,1
94,195,199,209,253]
    threshold, P [54,56]
Parking costs, P [191]
Pavlov, P [78]
Paying out of pocket, P [202]
Payment, P
[59,73,92,93,143,142,192,19
6,204.205,240, 241,245]
    agreement, P [204]
    types accepted, P
        [134]
PayPal, P [106]
Peace, P [41,88]
Personal, P
[7,12,13,26,27,35,37,41,81,8
9,90,91,92,98,103,112,114,12
3,132,142,164,176,177,181,1
82,193,195,198,209,247,253]
    image,
        P [98,123,164,247]
    trainer,
        P [37,142,209,253]
    training, P [112]
Personal Injury Protection
(PIP), P [92,132]
Personality types, P [50]
Philo Farnsworth, P [47]
Philosophy, P [218]
Photographer, P [136]
Photos, P [110,136]
Physical,

59,123,159,254]
Retail, P [106,214]
Rituals, P [735,36,149]
Robert Tisserand, P [73]
ROCKABYE BABY!, P [80]
Runners, P [224]

S

Saints, P [143,223,250]
Sauna, P [150]
Saviors, P [143]
Savvy, P [88,103,112,129,135,143]
Say "Yes!", P [151,152]
Scapula, P [22]
Schedule of availability, P [147]
Science, P [46,62,90]
Scientists, P [47]
Scope of practice, P [220]
Seated massage events, P [125]
Secrets of success, P [224]
Self, P[12,13,18,22,23,25,26,27,28 ,30,32,34,35,36,40,44,48,49,5 2,53,59,62,63,65,71,72,85,89, 92,93,96,98,102,103,108,110, 113,114,116,118,119,130,133 ,134,140,142,145,146,149,15 1,159,161,164,165,166,169,1 75,176,182,183,185,187,190, 193,208,217,223,224,230,233 ,235,240,242,245,247,249,25 0,251,252,253,255]
    care, P [35,36,110,149]

esteem, P [13,26,27,116]
    motivation, P [151]
    -compassion, P [96]
    -defeating voice, P [151]
    -forgiveness, P [96]
Sell, P [75,128,129,131,139,143,153 ,218,219]
    to your clients, P [153]
    your abilities, P [143]
Sensory, P [7,45,48,49,50]
Service providers, P [148]
Settling in court, P [198]
Sheepskin cover, P [184]
Shopping, P [87,105,150]
Sidney Jourard, P [145]
Six-figure income, P [111]
Small budget, P [137]
Snake oil selling, P [75]
Societal programming, P [152]
Sol, P [7,60,61,62]
Spa, P[10,34,49,87,107,125,139,1 63,166,215,218,227,230,231, 232,238]
    treatments, P [139,218]
Spasms, P [195]
Special offers, P [87]
Spine, P [51,137]
Sports treatment-oriented,

P [218]
Steuart Henderson Britt, P [121]
Stock photography, P [136]
Stop playing small, P [252]
Subconscious, P [46,79,128,131,138]
Success, P[5,8,10,12,13,16,17,18,21,28,32,35,40,46,50,59,68,75,98,100,101,102,115,116,117,118,122,124,131,137,138,144,146,147,149,151,154,169,173,190,213,214,216,217,222,224,226,230,231,239,250,251]
Successful business owner, P [149,217,239]
Super-fast service, P [131]
Surfer in a suit, P [10,252]
Swimming, P [37]
Symptoms, P[33,34,195,199,208,224,234]

T

Tai chi, P [37]
Tax write-off, P[86,192,138,242,243,245,146,247]
Teachers, P [47,143,145,250]
Techniques, P [8,37,38,55,58,93,94,102]
Technology, P [135]
Television, P [46,47,102,135,151,152]
Temporal region, P [51]
Tennis elbow, P [36,209]
Tension, P [46,57,195,245]
The good life, P [155]

Thumb, P [36]
Tiffany's, P [128]
Time, P[9,12,13,15,20,21,23,25,27,32,33,34,35,36,39,41,44,45,48,49,50,51,52,53,55,56,57,58,59,66,68,69,70,71,72,73,74,75,81,85,91,92,95,98,99,102,103,108,110,111,116,122,126,127,128,131,134,135,136,137,144,147,148,149,150,151,152,153,154,158,159,162,166,167,171,174,175,180,183,184,186,187,190,192,193,196,197,200,201,202,204,206,207,208,209,210,216,217,219,223,228,231,232,233,234,235,238,241,243,245,250,254,255]
Tip-offs, P [179]
Top dollar, P [26,192]
Touch, P[1,3,7,16,22,25,29,33,44,45,51,53,73,74,80,83,86,91,158,182,224]
Transportation costs, P [191]
Trauma, P [34,39,90,208,212]
Travel agents, P [142]
Treatment, P[15,22,25,26,28,36,37,52,53,56,70,76,82,115,139,142,158,159,167,178,179,192,193,194,195,197,198,201,202,203,206,207,208,209,210,211,215,218,219,220,221,222]
Twenty-hour workweek, P [150,218]
Two-year design program, P [129]

Other helpful, educational and inspiring books:

The Book of Massage: The Complete Stepbystep Guide to Eastern and Western Technique – Lucinda Lidell

Deep Tissue Massage, Revised: A Visual Guide to Techniques – Art Riggs and Thomas W. Meyers

Basic Clinical Massage Therapy: Integrating Anatomy and Treatment – James H. Clay and David M. Pounds

The Trigger Point Therapy Workbook: Your Self-treatment Guide for Pain Relief – Clair Davies, Amber Davies, and David G. Simons

Review for Therapeutic Massage and Bodywork Certification – Joseph Ashton and Duke Cassel

A Massage Therapist's Guide to Pathology – Ruth Werner

Mosby's Fundamentals of Therapeutic Massage – Sandy Fritz

Trigger Point Therapy for Myofascial Pain – Steven Finando

Start Your own Business – Rieva Lesonsky

If you're clueless about starting your own business – Seth Godin

Rich Dad Poor Dad – Robert Kiyosaki

The Seven Spiritual Laws of Success – Deepak Chopra

Success is not an Accident – Tommy Newberry

Unstoppable: 45 Powerful stories of Perseverance – Cynthia Kersey

The Four Agreements: A Practical Guide to Personal Freedom – Don Miguel Ruiz

ABOUT THE AUTHOR

Meagan Holub is committed to spreading health, wellness and the pursuit of happiness by all means necessary. She graduated from Seattle Massage School in 1995. In the latter half of her career she has been coined "Seattle's Celebrity Massage Therapist" because of her impressive client list.

She is currently owner of Hundred Thousand Dollar Massage and Spa Umi. Her philosophy is that anyone licensed in a healing art can make a six-figure income with dedication and an "out of the box" mind set. Her passion for writing was ignited as a child and after "The Magic Touch" book series and "Rubs to Riches" she hopes to write a memoir. She lives on a houseboat in Seattle with her tiny Pomeranian, Olive.

Her passions include: traveling to new and exotic places, an exquisite meal, high fashion, underground music, mid century modern design, massage, photography, independent film, volunteer work, and creating the life she loves. Not necessarily in that order.

She is available for consulting and seminars. You can find her contact information at www.hundredthousanddollarmassage.com.

RESOURCES

Direct links to products and services in the Magic Touch and
Meagan's seasonal selections can be found at
www.hundredthousanddollarmassage.com

Products

www.caycecures.com
www.amazon.com
www.shopbop.com
www.umiessentialorganics.mionegroup.com
www.revolveclothing.com
www.ebay.com
www.modernfurniture.com
www.islandthyme.com
www.zappos.com
www.moo.com

Services

www.imagroup.com
htdm@transfirst.com
www.ymca.net
www.cosmeticsdatabase.com
www.quotegarden.com

The world of massage is constantly evolving.
Stay on top of innovations and be involved in discussion forums at
Meagan's Rubs to Riches Blog found at
www.hundredthousanddollarmassage.com

Join our community of MTs and others committed to the health
And well-being of every individual on the planet!

CPSIA information can be obtained at www.ICGtesting.com
Printed in the USA
BVOW071513160912

300483BV00001B/62/P